maydust

Peter Anselm Garrelfs

Rock's Mills Press
Oakville, Ontario
2022

Published by
Rock's Mills Press
www.rocksmillspress.com

Illustrated by W. White
Original edition designed by W. White

For information about this book, including permissions re-
quests and retail and bulk orders, contact us at customer.
service@rocksmillspress.com or visit our website.

dedication

It is neither necessary nor desired, at least on my part, to be very explicit as to why or how creations, or perhaps the opposite, come about. It would be a mechanical dissection, a baking of clay into a form. I therefore humbly declare that I will discard whenever required, retain whenever useful, and abandon whenever necessary.

Many years have passed and blown words hither and thither. Time seems to have erased the last remnants of romanticism, never embraced to the fullest, or perhaps not even touched. No, the winds blow from another direction, compelling me to be as I am. Dreaming—yes, but rather broadly, about, or within, a vague linguistic jungle. Claims I make none, but rather cross the territory where such are made and violently defended. No, it was and is irrelevant to me.

Dedicated to you whose sun is rising, and to you whose sun is setting.

—Peter Anselm Garrelfs

To the One Who Knows

What else can I write to you?
My mouth is dry and the songs
of my yearning heart are echoing
in my poems and in long forgotten
lives of the past.

Like an old man, my footsteps echo
through the dry valley of uncried tears
and my eyes catch the sunrays
reflecting from the young springs
at the corners of my eyes.

A lost sheep seeking its shepherd
I call moaningly to the silence
and wait with thirsting mouth,
for the manna and rain to fall.

It is a voice calling without a sound
in the wilderness of my restless thoughts.

And yet here I am meandering in thought,
influenced by the vibrations of beautiful music,
which is thought—and yet, how much closer
to the cosmic rain of peace.

We seek happiness in the external world
and all we get is pleasure.
Is it not a sad, yet beautiful consolation
that happiness dwells within each and
every one of us—and it can be found.

The Lion's Roar

Curious he was and asked,
Demanding, knocking at the door.
A hand came down, removed his mask,
And made the lion roar.

How beautiful, and yet so black,
His heart absorbed the fire's beams.
A voice was heard and he crawled back,
Possessed by fearful dreams.

The lion grew and so did he;
His image had divided,
The lamb came down but there was she,
A roar and there was silence.

Curious he was and asked,
Demanding, knocking at the door.
Silence, and he felt the mask,
Surrounded by the lion's roar.

Long Ago and Now

Come then my children:
Let us play within the sandbox of creation.
You build the castles and I'll be the sand.

You have forgotten—
Searching madly in your forms and substances—
I never left.
And yet you do not know nor see.

My People

They come in rows and single file,
The lonely ones, the sad ones.
They smile in rows and single file,
The empty ones, the surface people.

The useless straw of surface people,
The dried-out words and phrases,
They drop the tears upon the straw,
The moisture of the sad ones.

To Be

Acknowledgement—
And then the human race began to be.
He picked it up, looked at it, and began to walk—
into misery.
It could have been me.
Why did he pick it up?
That miserable piece of nothing!

The Ditch Dweller

Oh is this hell to live in,
And heaven is so close.
The one is near, right in my mind,
The other deep within.

I look into your purple eyes,
Reflection of my own.
Desire in my knowledge lies,
Defeat deep down within.

Oh Masters, Angels, all of you,
Received in tales and dreams,
Where is the knowledge that I knew?
Where are your hands, your schemes?

Created by a force unknown,
The hammer slowly tears—
Away the fence protecting me
From sinking into earth.

I know, and yet I still do want
The fading love called world.
Oh please let pass that cup anon,
Instead, an angel's urge.

And as you react this, passerby,
Have compassion on my soul,
For when we meet in future time,
You might be in my role.

Whence?

And thus one wanders
From truth to illusion,
Inhaling the little light one finds.
Desires of man appear as truth,
According to one's understanding.
To the peasant the rain, the sun are gods,
To the philosopher, mere ideas.
Proclaiming avatars, messiahs alike
Declare the truth as asked,
For truth is one, not what we asked,
For that is but the answer.

The Nameless Man

Born he was, but he had no name.
The time—it's now—who is to blame?
He cries and fights for what—who knows!
For glamour and emptiness through this city blow.

From baby to child so fast he grew.
Tales of glamour, in the end not true,
Began to fill his heart with a dream,
His father in his eyes a god, his mother a queen.

The curtain went up—he was a man.
Desire and lust began to demand.
He gave in to them all but he lost his dream,
The city and people, how senseless they seem.

Eternity for him no longer exists,
The city is empty—what did he miss?
He walks through a hall all filled with gold,
Fur coats he wears but his core is cold.

He leaves the hall and comes to a tree,
Asking himself, "What's wrong with me?"
His eyes embrace the crown and the leaves.
The rays of the stars bring him some peace.

He returns to the hall to Gold and Cold,
With gambling and lust he tries to hold
That little warmth he received at the tree,
But time is passing—rapidly.

In place of water there is dust.
His laugh is only a hollow crust.
With a crutch under his arm, and almost blind,
He returns to the tree a second time.

The tree is there, so are the stars;
His eyes begin to feel the scars:
The ones he received while trying to hide
His search for peace and eternal light.

He goes down on his knees and begins to pray.
The hands of his trembling—he came a long way.
His eyes full of tears but at last he could see
His name written in the stem of the tree.

Back in the city, back in the hall,
They are playing and gambling, all of them all.
There is no purpose, there is no life;
Only nameless men, no love, no light.

Look at the people. Look at yourself.
Look at a book full of dust on your shelf.
Dust you are, and dust you shall be.
Can you see your name in the stem of the tree?

A Strange Jungle

O seeker on the path of light,
How many colours do you find?
How many people that got lost
Within the jungle of the Path?

Embracing their delusive fruits,
They seem to look at lamps of truth,
And only after years and years
Do they then realize and discover
That deep within there is a seed,
The wordless, soundless, ageless creed.

The Meek Man

And there it stands,
Its clubs all sorted out to swing.
Alas! Behold!
Upon the gang of moving human gloom.

And when one turns,
Pretending to be, 'happy meek man',
It checks its gear,
And hurls a club across the room.

Who is this 'It'?
With bulging eyes, a whirling fury
That cuts a path
Through meek man's death lament?

It must be he—
The one who turned and meekly smiled,
Pretending? Yes,
But is it real to life's demand?

The Fire Within

Caged in a flood of blood and sweat,
Crawling and running in miles of thought,
Utter confusion, utter delight
Turning around a thread.

To You

This is reaction kindly note,
Not action as it might appear
Observed through strictly human eyes,
Or otherwise as mankind wrote.

No, this is reinactivation,
Dormant within a soul of ice:
Created by inaction of reaction,
And yet a yearning heart within abides.

The Question

Am I too old to inscribe my mind
Upon the boundless stones?
Am I too young to end my life;
To cross the field of bones?

Lament

A ting, a bang, a ting, a bang,
We crawl from hill to hill,
Instead of looking toward the end,
We hold onto a string.

The waves they rise, the waves they fall,
And with them, so do we,
But where it leads, this all, this all,
It seems a useless thing.

One time we are a wave of joy,
The next time one of pain.
Identifying with it all,
We seem to lose the rein.

I call to you, I call to you,
In utter pain and joy.
Oh, how I yearn to be released,
And cease to be a toy.

Appointment with What?

Observing what one feels today,
The roaring sounds and hissing,
Emotions high, emotions low,
My God, what am I missing?

I searched the highway, searched the copse
And even rode the sky.
My head I put amongst the bees,
My feet into a pie.

Well George, let's face it, let's presume
The bees attacked your brain,
And while your feet did taste the pie,
Your hands did sign the claim.

And then you thought by gulping down,
You had attained the goal.
Oh gee-by-golly, what a folly,
You simply changed the role.

Instead of being what you were,
You are now split in two—
The one that serves that crackers, Folly,
The other, Mistress Woe.

The bees, they sting, the pies are sweet,
The hands keep signing claims,
And very soon among the rushes
You start collecting names.

You count and sign, continually sign,
And yet where is your gain?
You check your belly, pinch your button,
Exclaiming, it's the same.

The Mecca of Consideration

Such is life:
If it were any different
Man wouldn't want to know anything else.

If Man were born expecting not to be cheated
there would be a surprise.
If Man were born expecting to be cheated
there still would be a surprise.
Therefore, the man expecting both
has a lot to hope for.

Too much boredom produces staleness.
Too much activity a nervous wreck.
A little of both makes for a healthy,
bored individual.

Forgiveness in accordance with one's capacity
makes one grow, and healthy.
Too much forgiveness produces a nervous, broken
individual.

One can inflict or suffer a wound by
a word or an act.
But, true forgiveness does not bleed any longer.

Nothing is done without a reason.
Even the seeming absence of one does
not contradict that.

The Call

And thus a cry within a dream-world full of limitation
Aroused the parents' tender care and supplication

A baby born within the white-washed walls of desolation,
Creating thus a gimmick just before the fall.

The river's beckoning call of sparkling water,
Reflecting ancient pictures, crystal clear
—and dummies do the calls.

The green woods seem to hold the light of golden rays
And far beyond there lies the spring that started all
—this blurring call.

Oh where did life derive the strength to overcome
The muddy trenches that were encased in the hills of rocky stone.

The baby rides along the woolen hands of softique tissues,
And slowly it ascends the hill above the bend.

Oh yes—a curve was there, to tempt a sudden slide, below—
Into the valley, where massive food had just been carefully prepared.

Alas, above there lurks a cave where ancient hermits contemplated.
Perhaps they left behind a feeling for the hungry babe.

And as he twists his body through the crack within the walls
He leaves some skin behind—but still he didn't fall.

And when he looked and felt a shiver running up and down his spine,
He stretched his hand out—and again started crying.

Infinite

Do not criticize the ones that choose
to be hermits for my sake; for where
O man, can you go and not find me.

Do Not Despair

Beautiful indeed
appear the ways of all the many,
for utter loneliness
lurks where you are all by yourself.
Hallucinations many;
at first, at last, right to the end.
For them it is real, for you it is real,
and yet the end is different.

The Lonely Journey

To the clouds shall I go
To the wind will I speak
But your ears are deaf.

With the birds shall I fly
To the fish will I sing
But your sight is blinded.

Where do I go when I am lonely?

maydust

It

It craves and yearns for Its expression,
It wants to be released,
For if you had a mind possession
How could you be at peace.

Negation of Existence
According to them I am not to be
Beyond the land of thought and beings.
According to them I negate my being
If I do not accept this scheme.

However remote and vast a scheme,
It cannot be denied,
Beyond the land of thought and beings,
Reality begins and ends.

Return Within

No horizon, no boundaries,
No place to stand on,
Like a star in the sky,
Like a dream upon a cloud,
A bird swinging its wings,
A fish floating in the water.

Free you want to be
But only in your dreams
But only if you can reach beyond
Dare you don't know that you can't
You don't see the beautiful sun
You don't see the moon and the stars,
How beautiful
And they are part of you.

But you want to bring light into darkness
Without seeing yourself,
Dream and imagine that you are there
And you will learn to accept
—to live within yourself.

Musings

The moon is shining, the night is hot but peaceful, and I wish I were sitting somewhere in the country at a lake, or at the sea, watching the waves.

Looking at the stars, inhaling the air, inhaling peace and restlessness at the same time, dreaming of something which is indescribably beautiful, ugly, terrible; a thought impossible to put on paper, but it gives me peace.

I keep walking into the universe, into time which is no time, but still time, into the future, which is not future but future and past, circulating toward an end, or the end which is as much beginning as end.

But why live if end is beginning and beginning the end? But still it gives me peace; keeps me moving and searching and restless. Why?

There is no death but death.

Time is death and death is time.

But I keep on walking.

Walking into nothingness which is greatness as well; into fascinating beams of light, which become more and more light but at the same time are darkness. So dark and so light that at the end there is nothing but beginning and end, time and death. But I keep on walking. Why?

Reflection on Three

O Beauty, what a thought
Could enrapture thus my heart.
A peasant without wealth—
And yet, a man.
The tinkling bells of hours filled with joy,
Withdrawing into selflessness.
Where then indeed does joy express its beauty
If not within the deepfelt well of nothingness?
O what is strength, if not supported
By ancient columns deep within yourself?
And wisdom that so many vainly seek
Is but the ocean filled by many streams
We call experience.

Threshold

Watching while my eyes are closed,
Pretending that I hear.
Even though the door is closed,
My feelings are aware.

The hands they knock and also sound
The trumpet of the dawn.
And yet the silence reigns supreme,
The pictures are all gone.

Where are the flowers—red and white,
That seemed to hold the stage?
Where are thy thorns, O rose sublime,
That held you in your cage?

The light that filters through the door,
Upholding thus my faith,
Tells me the tales a hundredfold,
Submerging thus my haste.

And here I dwell, not moving yet
To wash the dust away.
Awaiting here the ray of light
That beckons not to sway.

Your Ideal I am

I am justice, comfort, trust and truth,
Of course the answer to your moves.
I am beauty, faith, a helping hand,
But most of all I am your friend.
I am love, yearning, light, real,
But most of all I am human,
For you made me your ideal.

Summer Winds

And on and on the winds blow gently,
Erasing footprints—all the trails.
The sand and dust spread out like waves,
Revealing beauty—hiding all.

O scenery beyond description,
Upon whose wings and many fictions,
The touch of summer winds so gently falls,
Revealing nothing—hiding all.

Love

Where are your dreams?
The dreams you had—it seems so long ago.
Mine—yes, and where are mine?
You sang with ardour like a nightingale
—with wings you flew across the abyss
—Life.
Oh Love eternal, love be mine—

Where are our dreams?
The dreams we had—not very long ago.
Ours—yes, where are they now?
We dreamt in unison like two-in-one
—with fins we swam across the ocean
—Life.
Oh Love eternal, Love be ours—

Where is it now?
Intangible—it seems without a shape or form.
It—yes, where is it now?
It changed the veils—many hiding one
—with charm it made the sceneries
—Life.
Oh Love eternal, Love be—

The Path

The smell, the breath, Oh how you feel it,
The long agos, the daffodillies.
The leaves of past are decomposing,
The twigs and stems—only memories.
And then as ashes turn to soil,
As young and urgent plants begin to coil,
Begin to grasp, to hold, to grow—
Oh then you know it's not in vain,
Your wants, your hopes, your scorching pains,
Your bitter nights of indecision,
The loneliness, the vastness of this mission
So small it be viewed from a safer distance.
And then as joy and hope through realization
Emerge upon the stage imagination,
As hate and love begin to merge,
Thus ending your eternal search,
As past and future blend together,
Thus giving you perhaps the final ladder—
Within the voidness of your being.

Tears

We walk through life upon the solid face of earth,
Constantly fighting, struggling to survive.
Beliefs we have, and yet they also struggle to survive.
We roam through splendid-ugly pictures in our minds;
Some call we good and some we see as bad.
Beliefs we have, and yet they also struggle to survive.
We fight with angels, demons, many beings,
In upper-lower regions of our minds.
Beliefs we have, and yet they also struggle to survive.
All Hope! A surge from deep within your being,
A stream of tears, that freely runs to purify,
While ego burns and slowly fades away
—no doors—no beings—only One.

Journey Into a Strange Land

Who called me forth to seek: and search
Within a land of thought and thought-creation?

Where milky pictures float behind,
Through gold and silvery doors.

A land where countless creatures form scenes
So strange and yet so beautiful.

Oh Lord, if you have given me eyes to see,
Let kindness move my tongue,
To paint the picture that your grace bestowed on me.

And so I roam through life, appearing full of suffering
Where mighty streams of foam and alleys full of disillusion,
Produce an eerie feeling full of loneliness.

If you imagine sitting in a crowd dumbfounded by a cinema production,
Could not then life be just the same—to what we call the gods?
If He, the One supreme in spirit expresses deep within
What we then see is but the likeness between steam and water.

Oh, if I could hold, and penetrate towards the centre,
The faces and the stories would be one.

How can I criticize and judge if all I see is but illusion to illusion
—and there behind it all there is but One?

And as I try to paint that which I know and feel within,
A sadness, like a serpent creeps upon my lonely path.

I see the Shu-As and the Hi-Tites deep within a form of milky foam.
It is a form and yet, a breeze coming from far beyond.

Oh, what I need now is the colour and the fragrance of the rose,
A dew-drop resting on the petals of its form.

Oh Father, please extend a loving thought
To comfort yet my frail and shaking hand,
So that I may express the Oneness of it all.

And as I travel, coming closer to the spring of light,
The useless pieces and the thoughts of agony and suffering
Become all rays, on which I ride toward the Sun.

Thought

And thus I do arrive—my tired feet set for Calcutta
To stretch my back upon the rubble of the street,
So crazily intertwined.

Where are the treasures I thought I could extract
From underneath the stench and steaming fog?
My eyes seem blinded by the flashing beams,
Reflecting on my unbelieving eyes.

And all the great ones that have cast their shadow
Imprinting their desires into man.

And thus my tired feet tread virgin soil,
Remaining thoughtless in the heart of virgin land.

Come

Treading feet, a pleasant sound,
A ray of light, or only light.
It is not I, but just my messengers in action.
Do sup with them; do drink a cup of joy.
But then my child—do hurry on.

The I

O man as I
Went on the journey
Perhaps a million years ago

O hear the I
It grew and faded
And still it held you until now.

O see the I
It crumbles slowly
Revealing thus the Truth—the Now.

Peter Anselm Garrelfs (August 1936–April 2021)
Son, brother, uncle, father, grandfather, friend
and poet

ABOUT THE AUTHOR

Peter Anselm Garrelfs was born in Germany in 1936, and lived through World War II as a child. Due to the horror, death and injustice he witnessed, Peter's poetry is deep, dark and introspective. Peter spent the majority of his adult life in Canada working outside of the arts in a rewarding career which allowed him to provide for his three children, but he never lost his great passion for music, writing and poetry. Peter died on April 29, 2021 with his children at his bedside. He will be greatly missed by his family and close friends; however, it is hoped that he will continue to share his love for life through the reissuing of this collection of his poetry.

CPSIA information can be obtained
at www.ICGtesting.com
Printed in the USA
LVHW110728120822
725756LV00004B/177

INTRODUCING MICROWAVE COMBINATION COOKERY

Jan Harris

ANGELL EDITIONS

Newton Abbot, Devon

Contents

Introduction   4
How your microwave combination oven works   4
Essential reading before you start cooking   4
Selecting the correct mode of cooking   4
Defrosting   5
Standing Time   5
Dishes Suitable for use in a combination oven   5
Measuring Ingredients   5

Soups   6

Fish   9

Meat   13

Poultry   20

Vegetables   24

Pasta, Rice and Cereals   29

Eggs and Cheese   34

Desserts   37

Cakes   45

Bread and Biscuits   50

Jams and Preserves   54

Sauces   57

Fruit   60

Index   63

Cover: Strawberry Affairé (page 41)

Gingerbread (page 45); Battenburg Cake (page 46)

Introduction

How Your Microwave Combination Oven Works

A combination oven is the result of marrying an electric fan oven with a microwave oven. To make the best use of your new oven it is necessary to understand how microwaves cook food. Microwaves are pulses of energy which are transmitted within the oven and cause the moisture molecules in food to vibrate. This vibration causes friction, which in turn creates heat, which cooks the food in the oven. Microwaves cannot penetrate metal so the interior of the oven is metal and the waves bounce off the walls in a figure of eight pattern into the food to be cooked. Since microwaves pass through glass or ceramic it is usual to cook in dishes made of a non-metallic substance. Please read page 5 carefully and refer to the instruction manual supplied with your machine.

It is often said that microwaves 'cook from the inside out' but this is just not true. Microwaves penetrate about 2cm (¾in) into food before being used up. Since there is no direct heat food does not brown when cooked by microwaves only and some found this limitation off-putting because dishes did not look cooked; though they were. The inclusion of a fan-assisted browning element means that a traditional crispy browned finish can be achieved combined with the speed and economy of energy that microwave cookery brings.

Essential Reading Before You Start Cooking

1. It is important that you know the out-put microwave power of your oven. The cooking times in this book are for ovens with 600/650 watts power out-put.
2. Microwave settings used in this book are High – Medium – Low – Defrost. Your oven may have different settings but it should be easy to relate them to those above.
3. Convection (fan-oven) settings used in this book are 160 degrees centigrade (160°C) to 250 degrees centigrade (250°C).

4. Following each recipe are cooking instructions abbreviated as the following example. Cook on microwave medium/combination 250° for 15 min.
5. It is sometimes necessary to pre-heat the oven using convection only where the short cooking time would not allow the oven to reach the required temperature to brown the dish before it is fully cooked. Where this is necessary the cooking instruction will specify as follows. Pre-heat the oven on convection 250° for 5 min.
6. Because of different manufacturing specifications and the variation from one oven to another it is impossible to specify exact cooking times. With practice, you will get to know your own oven.
7. Metal dishes may ONLY be used in your combination oven if specified in the manufacturer's instructions supplied with the oven. Remember that even when metal dishes are approved they can only be used for convection or combination cooking and NEVER on microwave only. If in doubt, use Pyrex but see page 5 where advice is given on dishes suitable for combination ovens.
8. As in conventional cooking it is sometimes necessary to cover dishes during cooking. When this is required it is stated in the recipe. Plastic wrap may be used to cover dishes when using microwave only and should normally be pierced to allow steam to escape. However, some brands of plastic wrap suitable for microwave cooking do not recommend piercing of the film because it splits. Be careful to avoid scalding steam when releasing this type of film. For convection or combination cooking, dishes should be covered with suitable conventional lids.

Selecting the Correct Mode of Cooking

Combination ovens usually have three options or choices available which are referred to as 'modes'.
1. Microwave only
2. Convection or fan-oven only
3. Combination – microwave and convection together

Some combination ovens also incorporate a grill.

The following information is for general

guidance. There are other uses for each mode which you will learn from experience.

Combination: roast meats, Yorkshire pudding, roast potatoes, scalloped potatoes and other gratin dishes, pastries, cakes, bread, fruit crumbles. Any food which needs a crisp or crusty brown top or finish.

Convection only: is most frequently used for pre-heating the oven prior to combination cooking. It is also used for baking such as fairy cakes where combination cooking would be too quick to allow browning to take place. Serving plates can also be warmed in the traditional way.

Microwave only: vegetables, fruit, sauces, milk puddings, rice, pasta, scrambled and poached eggs, chutneys, jam, marmalade, lemon curd, fish, beefburgers, bacon, chicken portions, re-heating, defrosting, melting chocolate, jelly cubes, butter, margarine and cooking fats.

Defrosting

The defrost facility enables the combination oven to be used in conjunction with a freezer to great benefit. Pre-cooked food can be defrosted and heated quickly when needed or impromptu meals cooked using meat, poultry or fish from the freezer, with the minimum of delay. The most common fault when using the microwave mode to defrost is 'over-defrosting' which means that the food has started to cook on the outside whilst remaining frozen in the middle. A period of standing or resting time during defrosting will help to overcome this problem.

Standing Time

Standing time mainly applies to food cooked on microwave-only mode. It is particularly important when food, such as vegetables, has a critical cooking time. The food continues to cook after it has been removed from the oven because the friction caused by the microwaves continues to create heat. Microwaves are used up instantly they enter food so there is no danger of any being left after the oven has switched itself off. Another example of when standing time is important is in the baking of cakes using micro-wave only. It is necessary to stop cooking when the cake is slightly moist in the centre otherwise it will overcook during the standing time and be too dry.

Dishes Suitable for Use in a Combination Oven

The best choice is Pyrex or earthenware, which has been manufactured for use in a microwave oven, since they can be used during all modes of cooking. If you are in doubt about the suitability of a piece of earthenware it can be tested for efficiency by adding water and microwaving on Full for a minute or two. If the dish gets hot before the water then it is unsuitable for use in a microwave oven. Do remember that all dishes will get hot during cooking, even on microwave-only mode and this is due to heat transference from the food to the dish. You will need to use oven gloves just as with an ordinary oven.

Plastics: There are new plastic dishes available which can be used in a combination oven but normal plastic dishes will melt if used during combination or convection modes. Since micro-waves pass through plastic it is permissible to use plastic containers when cooking on the microwave mode but do remember that the temperature of the food might melt the plastic. Whilst it is fine for reheating a portion of stew it would melt if used in jam-making where the temperature is extremely high.

Glass: Toughened glass such as Pyrex is ideal for all modes but ordinary glass is risky since the temperature of the food might cause it to crack.

Metal: Metal dishes may be used in SOME microwave combination ovens but NOT in others. It is essential to check the manufacturer's instructions issued with your machine before using metal dishes on combination mode. Under no circumstances should metal be used on microwave-only mode since microwaves cannot penetrate metal and it could damage the magnetron in the oven. Do not leave metal spoons or whisks in the oven during cooking. Avoid gold or silver edged dishes during micro-wave cooking since the decoration is metal.

Measuring Ingredients

Both metric and imperial measures are given throughout the book. It is important to weigh and measure accurately and choose which standard you prefer. Do not mix metric and imperial measurements during the preparation of recipes. All spoon measures are level unless otherwise specified.

Soups

Home-made soups are warming on winter days and taste so much better than packet or tinned varieties. The number of servings are given with each recipe but it is easy to double or half the quantities as required. Just remember that the cooking time will increase with the volume. Soup can be made in advance and stored in the freezer until needed. Good stock can be made from a chicken carcase or ham bones but stock cubes are a convenient alternative. It is much quicker to boil water in an electric kettle than to heat large quantities in a microwave oven. Use leftover vegetables added to hot stock and liquidised to make a tasty soup. The possibilities are limitless.

French onion soup *(serves 4)*

50g (2oz) butter
450g (1lb) large onions, sliced thinly
1 teaspoon caster sugar
2 teaspoons flour
1l (1½pt) hot beef stock
salt and pepper
4 slices french bread
50g (2oz) grated cheddar cheese

1 Melt the butter in a large casserole on microwave high for 1 min.
2 Add the onions and stir to coat in the melted butter.
3 Cook, covered, on microwave high for 5 min. Stir occasionally.
4 Stir in the sugar and cook on microwave high for 2 min.
5 Blend in the flour and gradually stir in the hot stock. Season with salt and pepper.
6 Cook, covered, on microwave high for 12 min. Stir occasionally.
7 Lightly toast the bread and sprinkle with the grated cheese.
8 Float the slices of bread on the soup and return to the oven. Cook on microwave high for 3 min or until the cheese has melted.

Quick minestrone soup *(serves 4)*

1 tin of Spring vegetable soup
600ml (1pt) hot water
1 small tin baked beans in tomato sauce
1 tablespoon tomato purée
1 clove garlic, crushed
50g (1oz) macaroni
salt and pepper
parmesan cheese, grated

1 Combine all the ingredients, except the cheese, in a large casserole.
2 Cook, covered, on microwave high for 20 min or until the macaroni is soft. Stir occasionally.
3 Serve in individual bowls and garnish with grated parmesan cheese.

Chunky chicken soup *(serves 2)*

1 large chicken portion or ½ chicken
1 small turnip
1 small swede
1 medium parsnip
1 leek
1 medium onion
2 carrots
15g (½oz) butter
450ml (¾pt) hot chicken stock
salt and pepper
1 teaspoon cornflour

1 Remove skin from the chicken.
2 Chop all the prepared vegetables.
3 Except for the cornflour, combine all the ingredients in a large casserole. Ensure that the chicken is covered by the stock and vegetables.
4 Cook, covered, on microwave high for 15 min.
5 Stir and cook, covered, on microwave low/simmer for 30 min.
6 Mix the cornflour with a little water and stir into the soup.
7 Cook on microwave high for 2 min or until the soup has thickened.
8 Stir well and remove bones before serving.

Note: *This soup is an ideal way of using a chicken carcase with boiling water replacing the stock.*

Quick Minestrone Soup (above)

Cream of tomato soup *(serves 2)*

800g (1lb 12oz) tin tomatoes
300ml (½pt) boiling water
1 tablespoon demerara sugar
½ teaspooon Worcester sauce
50g (2oz) unsalted butter
300ml (½pt) double cream

1 Chop the tomatoes and retain the juice.
2 Combine all the ingredients, except the butter and double cream, in a large casserole.
3 Cook, covered, on microwave high for 14 min. Stir occasionally.
4 Allow to cool slightly and press through a sieve.
5 Return the purée to a clean casserole and stir in the butter.
6 Cook, covered, on microwave high for 2 min.
7 Gently whisk in the double cream and heat on microwave high for 2 min.
8 Serve hot or cold garnished with a swirl of single cream and chopped parsley.

Note: *Do not allow to boil after adding the cream. Fresh, ripe tomatoes may be used instead of tinned tomatoes but increase the boiling water to 600ml (1pt).*

Lentil soup *(serves 4)*

150g (6oz) lentils
1.2 litres (2pt) hot ham stock
50g (2oz) butter
1 large onion, chopped
2 large carrots, chopped
1 bouquet garni
3 tablespoons double cream
salt and pepper

1 Combine all the ingredients in a large casserole and cook, covered, on microwave high for 30 min or until the lentils and vegetables are soft.
2 Remove the bouquet garni.
3 Allow to cool slightly and liquidise or press through a sieve.
4 Adjust seasoning.
5 Cook, covered, on microwave high for 4 min or until hot.

Mushroom soup *(serves 2)*

225g (8oz) mushrooms
1 medium onion
100g (4oz) butter
100g (4oz) self-raising flour
300ml (½pt) hot chicken stock
salt and pepper
150ml (¼pt) single cream

1 Slice the mushrooms very finely and chop the onion.
2 Melt the butter in a large casserole on microwave high for 2 min.
3 Add the mushrooms and onion and stir to coat with the melted butter.
4 Cook, covered, on microwave high for 5 min.
5 Blend the flour with a little of the stock until smooth.
6 Add this to the mushroom mixture and stir well.
7 Stir in the remainder of the stock and season with salt and pepper.
8 Cook, covered, on microwave high for 4 min.
9 Allow the soup to cool slightly and liquidise or press through a sieve.
10 If necessary re-heat on microwave high.
11 Serve garnished with a swirl of single cream and a sprig of watercress or a few slices of raw mushrooms.

Fish

Although fish is a valuable source of nutrients the doubts about freshness and the cooking smells created have put many people off its preparation. Your microwave oven will enable you to defrost frozen fish quickly and safely and the very short cooking times virtually eliminate odours in the kitchen. You will also find that fish cooked in the microwave oven retains its flavour and natural juices provided that you do not overcook it. It is better to slightly undercook fish because it will continue to cook during the standing time which occurs before serving.

Fish fingers

6 frozen fish fingers

1 Pre-heat the oven on convection 250° for 5 min.
2 Arrange the fish fingers on the rack in the oven.
3 Cook on combination 250°/microwave medium for 3 min.

Note: *For a crisper finish brush the fish fingers with oil prior to cooking.*

Breaded plaice fillets

450g (1lb) breaded plaice fillets

1 Pre-heat the oven on convection 250° for 5 min.
2 Arrange the fish fillets on the rack in the oven.
3 Cook on combination 250°/microwave medium for 4 min.

Note: *If frozen fish is used cook for 8 min. For a crisper finish brush with oil prior to cooking.*

Kippers

450g (1lb) kippers

1 Place the kippers in a casserole.
2 Cover and cook on microwave high for 6 min.

Note: *If frozen fish is used cook for 8 minutes.*

Fish cakes

450g (1lb) cooked white fish with skin and bones removed
350g (12oz) creamed potatoes
50g (2oz) fresh breadcrumbs
1 egg
2 tablespoons chopped parsley
salt and pepper

for the coating
seasoned flour
2 eggs, lightly beaten
crisped golden breadcrumbs

1 Flake the cooked fish and pick over for bones.
2 In a large bowl combine the fish, potatoes, breadcrumbs, egg and parsley. Season to taste and stir well.
3 Form into 12 fishcakes of even size.
4 Chill in the refrigerator for 15 min.
5 Coat each fishcake in the seasoned flour, then the beaten egg and finally, the golden breadcrumbs.
6 Pre-heat the oven on convection 250° for 5 min.
7 Place, six at a time, on the rack in the oven and cook on combination 250°/microwave medium for 6 min.

Note: *For a crisper finish brush the fishcakes with oil prior to cooking.*

VARIATION
Substitute tinned tuna or salmon for white fish and halve the quantities of the other ingredients to make 6 fishcakes.

Stuffed trout

2×225g (8oz) trout, cleaned and gutted but heads and tails left on
2 tablespoons grated carrot
1 stick celery, finely chopped
1 small eating apple, peeled, cored and finely chopped
2 teaspoons chopped onion
salt and pepper

1 Pierce the skin of the fish in several places with a sharp knife to prevent bursting during cooking.
2 Place the trout head to tail on an oval plate.
3 Combine the ingredients for the stuffing in a bowl. Stir well and season to taste.
4 Stuff the fish with the mixture and arrange any excess around the trout.
5 Cook on microwave high for 9–10 min.

Note: *You may protect the tails and eyes with small pieces of smooth foil which is removed after cooking. Do not allow foil to touch the interior of the oven.*

Moules marinière

600ml (1pt) mussels
25g (1oz) butter
1 small onion, finely chopped
1 clove garlic, crushed
150ml (¼pt) dry white wine
freshly ground black pepper
single cream

1 Wash and scrub the mussels, discarding any that are open.
2 Melt the butter in a casserole on microwave high for 1 min.
3 Stir in the onion and garlic and cook on microwave high for 2 min or until the onions are soft.
4 Add the wine and season with black pepper.
5 Return the dish to the oven and heat on microwave high until the liquid boils.
6 Add the mussels and cook on microwave high for a minimum of 3 min or until the shells open.
7 Drain well and discard any unopened shells.
8 Serve, steaming hot, in an open dish with single cream swirled over the uppermost shells.

Haddock bake

350g (¾lb) haddock fillets
2 teaspoons chopped parsley
salt and pepper
300ml (½pt) thick cheese sauce (see page 58)
50g (2oz) grated cheese

1 Place the fish evenly across the base of a buttered rectangular pie dish.
2 Sprinkle the chopped parsley over the fish and season well with salt and pepper.
3 Pour on the cheese sauce and sprinkle with the grated cheese.
4 Pre-heat the oven on convection 250° for 5 min.
5 Place the dish on the rack in the oven and cook on combination 250°/microwave medium for 10 min. If a more brown look is wanted continue to cook on convection 250° for 8 min or until satisfactory.

Cod in parsley sauce

225g (8oz) cod, filleted and skinned
salt and pepper
450ml (¾pt) white sauce (see page 57)
1 tablespoon chopped parsley

1 Place the fish in the bottom of a buttered, oval pie dish and season with salt and pepper.
2 Stir the chopped parsley into the white sauce and pour over the fish.
3 Cook on microwave high, uncovered, for 4–5 min.

Stuffed Trout (above); Moules Marinière (above)

Fish pie

350g (¾lb) skinned and filleted white fish
25g (1oz) butter
150ml (¼pt) thick white sauce (see page 58)
150ml (¼pt) fish stock or water
75g (3oz) peeled prawns
900g (2lb) creamed potatoes

1 Place the fish in a casserole and dot with half the butter.
2 Cover and cook on microwave high for 4 min.
3 Drain. Flake the fish removing any bones.
4 Add the white sauce, stock, prawns and half the creamed potatoes. Mix well.
5 Spread the remaining creamed potatoes over the mixture and dot with the remaining butter.
6 Pre-heat the oven on convection 250° for 5 min.
7 Place the dish on the rack in the oven and cook on convection 250° for 20 min or until the top is golden brown.

Prawn curry

225g (8oz) diced mixed vegetables
1 large onion, chopped
15g (½oz) butter
1 medium tin chopped tomatoes
1 tablespoon Madras curry powder
1 tablespoon demerara sugar
1 tablespoon tomato puree
1 tablespoon chutney
1 bay leaf
salt and pepper
100g (4oz) peeled prawns

1 Combine the mixed vegetables, onion and butter in a casserole.
2 Cover and cook on microwave high for 7 min.
3 Add the remainder of the ingredients, except the prawns. Stir well and season to taste.
4 Cover and cook on microwave medium for 20 mins.
5 Add the prawns and stir gently.
6 Cook on microwave medium for 9 min.
7 Remove the bay leaf and serve.

Seafood thermidor

100g (4oz) crabmeat
100g (4oz) mashed potato
50g (2oz) peeled prawns or shrimps
150ml (¼pt) fish stock
3 tablespoons dry white wine
1 teaspoon tomato puree
½ teaspoon French mustard
1 tablespoon double cream
salt and pepper
25g (1oz) grated cheese

1 Combine all the ingredients, except the grated cheese, in a bowl.
2 Season to taste and stir well.
3 Place the mixture in a buttered oval pie dish and sprinkle the grated cheese on top.
4 Pre-heat the oven on convection 250° for 5 min.
5 Place the dish on the rack in the oven and cook on convection 250° for 8 min or until the cheese has melted and turned golden brown.

Meat

Perhaps the biggest disappointment for users of microwave ovens was the traditional Sunday roast. Roast beef could not be brown and crisp outside and pink in the middle and Yorkshire pudding was one of the few dishes that could not be attempted. Critics of microwave ovens frequently pointed out these shortcomings and many people were wrongly persuaded that there was not a place for a microwave oven in their kitchens. No such problems occur with a combination oven. Roast beef can be cooked exactly to your taste with less reduction of the joint and fuel economy as well. Yorkshire pudding is no longer a problem. In fact your combination oven will give you the best of traditional cooking methods with the speed of microwave, where appropriate.

Beef stew

450g (1lb) stewing or braising steak
2 carrots
1 small turnip
1 parsnip
½ small swede
1 medium onion
1 leek
600ml (1pt) hot beef stock
salt and pepper
plain flour

1 Trim any fat off the meat and cut into cubes.
2 Roughly chop all the prepared vegetables.
3 Combine the meat and vegetables in a 2½ litre (4pt) casserole. Stir in the stock and season with salt and pepper.
4 Cook, covered, on microwave high for 8 min.
5 Stir, and continue to cook, covered, on microwave low/simmer for 1 hour 45 min or until the meat is tender.
6 To thicken, blend a little flour with some of the stock and gradually add to the stew stirring continuously to avoid lumps.
7 Cook, covered on microwave high for 3 min.

Dumplings

150g (6oz) plain flour
75g (3oz) suet

1 Mix the ingredients adding sufficient water to form a soft dough.
2 Form into 6 dumplings.
3 Add to hot stew and cook, covered, on microwave high for 5–6 min.

Braised beef with onions

450g (1lb) lean braising steak
50g (2oz) plain flour
salt and pepper
225g (½lb) onions, sliced
450ml (¾pt) hot beef stock

1 Trim any fat off the meat and cut into cubes.
2 Season the flour in a polythene bag.
3 Add the meat, a few pieces at a time, and shake well to coat.
4 Make a layer with the onions in a 1.2 litre (2pt) casserole.
5 Make a layer of the coated meat over the onions.
6 Pour over the stock.
7 Cook, covered, on microwave high for 10 min. Continue to cook, covered, on microwave low/simmer for 1 hour or until the meat is tender.

Note: *The quality of the braising steak will determine the cooking time. If additional cooking is required it may be necessary to add further stock.*

Beefburgers

4 frozen beefburgers

1 Pre-heat the oven on convection 250° for 5 min.
2 Place the beefburgers on the rack in the oven and cook on combination 250°/microwave medium for 3 min.

Note: *If preferred, cooking oil may be brushed over the beefburgers prior to cooking.*

Quick chilli con carne

450g (1lb) minced beef
1 beef stock cube, crumbled
400g (14oz) tin chopped tomatoes
150g (6oz) tin kidney beans, drained
1 packet chilli con carne mix

1 Cook the mince in a covered casserole on microwave high for 5 min.
2 Drain off any fat and break up the mince with a fork.
3 Stir in all the other ingredients.
4 Cook, covered, on microwave high for 20 min. Stir every 5 min.

Note: *1–2 teaspoons chilli powder can be used instead of the chilli con carne mix.*

Roast beef

The quality of the joint will determine the cooking time. Top quality meat can be cooked quickly but cheaper cuts should be cooked at a lower temperature for longer. If a joint contains a large bone the cooking time must be reduced to compensate. The following times are a guide but do remember that it is better to undercook for those who like their beef rare and cook sliced meat on microwave high for 1 min or longer for those who prefer it well done. In all cases pre-heat the oven on convection 250° for 5 min and place the joint on the rack in the oven.

Sirloin, topside etc. - Rare 7–8 min per 450g (1lb). Medium 10 min per 450g (1lb) cooked on combination 250°/microwave medium.

Brisket, etc. - 15 min per 450g (1lb) on combination 220°/microwave medium.

To roast potatoes, place them on the trivet directly below the joint and the fat dripping off the meat will baste them. If you are cooking a small joint potatoes may be cooked for the full time but for a large joint add the potatoes half way through the cooking cycle. It will be necessary to add 5 min per 450g (1lb) of potatoes to the total cooking time.

Note: *If the joint has very little fat it is advisable to brush with oil prior to cooking.*

Yorkshire pudding

100g (4oz) plain flour
good pinch salt
1 egg, size 3
300ml (½pt) milk

1 Combine the flour and salt in a mixing bowl.
2 Make a well in the centre of the flour and add the egg.
3 Mix well, gradually adding half the milk.
4 Mix until smooth and beat for 1 min.
5 Gently stir in the rest of the milk.
6 Pour the batter into a lightly oiled 600ml (1pt) rectangular dish.
7 Pre-heat the oven on convection 250° for 5 min.
8 Place the dish on the rack in the oven and cook, uncovered, on combination 250°/ microwave medium for 13 min.

Note: *A mixture of half milk, half water may be used if preferred. If roast beef has just been cooked it will not be necessary to pre-heat the oven.*

Shepherd's pie

450g (1lb) minced beef
1 medium onion, chopped
450ml (¾pt) hot beef stock
salt and pepper
450g (1lb) creamed potatoes

1 Cook the mince and onion together in a covered casserole on microwave high for 5 min.
2 Drain off any fat and break up the mince with a fork.
3 Add the stock and seasoning and cook, covered, on microwave high for 13 min.
4 Pour the mince into a 1.2 litre (2pt) oval pie dish and spread the creamed potatoes evenly over the surface. Use a fork to neaten the top.
5 Pre-heat the oven on convection 250° for 5 min.
6 Place the dish on the rack in the oven and cook, uncovered, on convection 250° for 10 min, or until the potato top is brown.

Roast Beef (above); Yorkshire Pudding (above); Carrots (page 24)

Cheshire hot pot

450g (1lb) lean chuck steak
25g (1oz) beef dripping
4 large potatoes, thinly sliced
3 large carrots, sliced
1 large onion sliced
600ml (1pt) hot beef stock
salt and pepper

1 Trim any fat off the meat and cut into cubes.
2 Melt the dripping on microwave high for approximately ½ min.
3 Use a little of the melted fat to grease a 3 litre (5pt) casserole.
4 Make a layer of potato and season lightly.
5 Continue to make layers of beef, carrot, onion and potato. Lightly season each layer. Finish with a neat layer of potatoes.
6 Pour the stock over and top with the melted dripping.
7 Cook, covered, on microwave high for 15 min.
8 Continue to cook, covered on microwave low/simmer for 1 hour 15 min.

Steak and kidney pudding

450g (1lb) prepared steak and kidney
300ml (½pt) hot beef stock (made with 1 beef stock cube)
150g (6oz) self-raising flour
75g (3oz) shredded suet
salt and pepper

1 Mix the meat with the stock in a 1.2 litre (2pt) casserole.
2 Cook, covered, on microwave high for 5 min.
3 Stir and continue to cook, covered, on microwave low/simmer for 1 hour 30 min.
4 Mix together the flour and suet with sufficient water to form a stiff dough.
5 Roll-out the dough on a floured surface to line a greased 1.2 litre (2pt) pudding basin, reserving enough dough for a lid to cover the basin.

6 Fill the dough-lined basin with meat and stock.
7 Sprinkle with salt and pepper and a little flour.
8 Dampen the edge of the dough and add the lid. Press to seal the edge.
9 Cover with plastic wrap and use a sharp knife to slit through the plastic wrap and dough lid to allow air to escape.
10 Cook on microwave high for 6 min.

Savoury minced beef

450g (1lb) lean minced beef
1 medium onion, chopped
400g (14oz) tin chopped tomatoes
225g (8oz) diced mixed vegetables, fresh or frozen
450ml (¾pt) hot beef stock
salt and pepper

1 Mix together the mince and onion in a 1.2 litre (2pt) casserole.
2 Cook, covered, on microwave high for 6 min.
3 Drain off any fat and break-up the mince with a fork.
4 Add the remaining ingredients and seasoning. Stir well.
5 Cook, covered, on microwave high for 14 min or until the vegetables are tender.

Lamb chops

4×125g (5oz) lamb chops
salt and pepper

1 Pre-heat the oven on convection 250° for 5 min.
2 Season the chops with salt and pepper
3 Place the chops on the rack in the oven and cook, uncovered, on combination 250°/microwave medium for 6 min for medium cooked lamb. Adjust the time for pink or well done.

Note: *Additional browning can be achieved by further cooking on convection 250° for 5 min or longer.*

Roast lamb

Follow the same instructions as for roast beef (see page 14) but allow 9 min per 450g (1lb) on combination 220°/microwave medium for shoulder or leg and 11 min for cheaper cuts. Rosemary may be used to flavour the lamb during cooking.

Roast crown of lamb

2kg (4lb) prepared crown of lamb
225g (8oz) made-up stuffing
salt and pepper

1 Remove the turntable from the oven and place the crown of lamb in the centre.
2 Spoon the stuffing into the centre of the crown.
3 Season with salt and pepper.
4 Pre-heat the oven on convection 220° for 5 min.
5 Return the turntable to the oven and cook, uncovered, on combination 220°/microwave medium for approximately 20 min for medium cooked lamb. Adjust the time for pink or well done.

Note: *If your oven has a separate trivet use it instead of the turntable.*

Gammon steaks with pineapple

2×225g (8oz) gammon steaks
2 pineapple rings
salt and pepper

1 Trim excess fat and snip edges to prevent curling.
2 Season with salt and pepper and place pineapple rings on the steaks.
3 Pre-heat the oven on convection 250° for 5 min.
4 Place the steaks on the rack in the oven and cook, uncovered, on combination 250°/microwave medium for 4 min.
5 Remove the pineapple and turn the steaks over. Replace the pineapple and continue cooking for a further 3–4 min.

Pork chops

4×125g (5oz) pork chops
salt and pepper

1 Cut through the skin and fat of each chop in several places to prevent curling during cooking.
2 Season with salt and pepper.
3 Pre-heat the oven on convection 250° for 5 min.
4 Place the chops on the rack in the oven and cook on combination 250°/microwave medium for 7 min.

Note: *If preferred, the chops may be brushed with oil prior to cooking. Additional browning can be achieved by additional cooking on convection 250° for 5 min or longer.*

Sausages

450g (1lb) sausages

1 Pre-heat the oven on convection 250° for 5 min.
2 Place the sausages on the rack in the oven and cook, uncovered, on combination 250°/microwave medium for 4 min.
3 Cook on convection 250° for 10 min or until sausages are brown. Turn after 5 min.

Frozen sausage rolls

1 packet of 6 large frozen sausage rolls
1 egg, beaten

1 Remove the rack from the oven.
2 Pre-heat the oven on convection 250° for 5 min.
3 Place the sausage rolls, seam down, on the rack and brush with the beaten egg.
4 Cook, uncovered, on combination 250°/microwave medium for 5 min or until suitably brown.

Roast ham

1×900g (2lb) joint roasting ham
cooking oil
salt and pepper

1 Score the ham skin with a sharp knife.
2 Brush with cooking oil and season well with salt and pepper.
3 Pre-heat the oven on convection 250° for 5 min.
4 Place the ham on the rack in the oven and cook, uncovered, on combination 250°/microwave medium for 16 min or until cooked through.

Note: *It is advisable to soak ham joints overnight in cold water to remove any excess salt. For larger joints cook on combination 220°/microwave medium for 10 min per 450g (1lb).*

Bacon rashers

225g (½lb) bacon rashers

1 Place the rashers on the rack in the oven.
2 Cook, uncovered, on microwave high for 1 min per rasher.
3 If crispy bacon is preferred, turn the rashers and continue to cook for 1 min or longer.

Note: *To prevent splashing, cover the rashers with kitchen paper but remove immediately cooking is finished otherwise it will stick to the bacon.*

Savoury bacon rolls

8 rashers streaky bacon
225g (8oz) prepared sage and onion stuffing
8 wooden cocktail sticks

1 Remove the rind from the bacon.
2 Divide the stuffing into 8 portions.
3 Wrap each portion of stuffing in a bacon rasher.
4 Secure each bacon roll with a cocktail stick.
5 Arrange on the rack in the oven and cook, uncovered, on microwave high for 9 min.

Ham layer pudding

50g (2oz) mushrooms, chopped
2 spring onions, chopped
100g (4oz) cooked ham, diced
2 teaspoons dried mixed herbs
50g (2oz) shredded suet
100g (4oz) self-raising flour
3 tablespoons milk
15g (½oz) butter
garlic salt – optional
salt and pepper

1 Mix together the mushrooms, spring onions, ham and herbs.
2 Make a soft dough with the suet, flour and milk.
3 Roll-out on a floured surface to make 2×15cm (6in) circles.
4 Cut 1 circle into 4 wedges.
5 Divide the ham mixture into 3 portions and sprinkle 1 portion into a greased 1.2 litre (2pt) pudding basin.
6 Place 2 of the dough segments on top to form a layer.
7 Season with garlic salt, if used and salt and pepper. Dot with a little of the butter.
8 Make a further layer of ham mixture and a further layer of dough segments. Season and dot with butter.
9 Make a final layer of ham mixture and top with the complete dough circle.
10 Cover with plastic wrap and cook on microwave high for 5 min.

Note: *Chopped cooked streaky bacon can be substituted for the ham.*

Ham Layer Pudding (above); Roast Ham (above); Boiled Potatoes (page 24)

Poultry

Chicken is no longer a luxury and is cheaper than most other meat. It is also low in cholesterol to meet today's demands for more healthy eating. Fortunately, chicken can be cooked in many different ways to give variety and excitement to everyday meals as well as special occasions.

Spicy chicken

50g (2oz) flour
½ teaspoon ground ginger
¾ teaspoon salt
½ teaspoon pepper
1 clove garlic, crushed
4×225g (8oz) chicken joints, skinned
1 egg, beaten
½ teaspoon oregano
½ teaspoon paprika
3 tablespoons chives, chopped
½ teaspoon curry powder
450ml (¾pt) hot chicken stock
12 silverskin onions, cooked

1 Mix together the flour, ginger, salt, pepper and garlic.
2 Brush the chicken joints with beaten egg.
3 Roll each joint in the seasoned flour. Reserve flour not used.
4 Place the joints in a greased, 1.5 litre (3pt) circular Pyrex dish.
5 Cook, uncovered, on combination 250°/microwave medium for 10 min.
6 Combine all the remaining ingredients, except the onions, in a jug with the hot chicken stock.
7 Sprinkle the reserved seasoned flour over the chicken and add the stock.
8 Cook, uncovered, on combination 250°/microwave medium for 16 min.
9 Stir in the silverskin onions and cook on microwave high for 2 min.

Chicken casserole

3 tablespoons plain flour
salt and pepper
4×175g (7oz) chicken portions, skinned
3 sticks celery
3 medium carrots, sliced
1 medium onion, chopped
400g (14oz) tin chopped tomatoes
300ml (½pt) hot chicken stock
50g (2 oz) button mushrooms

1 Season the flour with salt and pepper.
2 Coat the chicken portions in the flour.
3 Place the portions in a casserole, smooth side up.
4 Add the vegetables and pour the stock over.
5 Place the dish on the rack in the oven and cook, covered, on combination 250°/microwave medium for 30 min.
6 Take the dish from the oven and put the chicken pieces on top of the vegetables.
7 Return to the oven and cook, uncovered, on combination 250°/microwave medium for 10 min or until the chicken is nicely browned.

Roast chicken

1 oven-ready chicken
2 tablespoons cooking oil
salt and pepper

1 Pierce the skin several times with a fork
2 Brush with oil and season with salt and pepper.
3 Pre-heat the oven on convection 250° for 5 min.
4 Place the chicken directly on the rack in the oven and cook on combination 250°/microwave medium. For birds up to 2 kg (4.4lb) cook for 9 min per 450g (1lb) and 7 min per 450g (1lb) for heavier birds.

Note: *The weight calculation should include stuffing, if used.*

Roast chicken breasts

4×350g (12oz) chicken breasts with skins and
  bones left in
1 tablespoon cooking oil
salt and pepper

1 Pre-heat the oven on convection 250° for 5
min.
2 Brush the chicken breasts with oil and season
well.
3 Place directly on the rack in the oven and
cook on combination 250°/microwave medium
for 10–12 min.

Note: *To cook chicken legs or wings follow the same
procedure but cook for 10–12 min per 450g (1lb).*

Chicken fricassée

100g (4oz) butter
8 shallots, peeled
150g (6oz) carrots, sliced into rounds
75g (3oz) mushrooms, sliced
4×275g (10oz) chicken joints, skinned
50g (2oz) plain flour, seasoned
60ml (2fl oz) dry white wine
200ml (7fl oz) chicken stock
1 bouquet garni
2 bay leaves
4 tablespoons double cream

1 Melt the butter in a 2.5 litre (3pt) casserole
on microwave high for 2 min.
2 Add the shallots and carrots and spoon the
melted butter over to coat.
3 Cook on microwave high, uncovered, for 10
min.
4 Stir in the mushrooms and cook, uncovered,
for a further 2 min.
5 Use a slotted spoon to remove the vegetables
from the dish. Reserve.
6 Coat the chicken pieces in the seasoned
flour and reserve the rest of the flour.
7 Add the chickens to the dish and coat in the
melted butter.
8 Cook, covered, on combination 250°/
microwave medium for 14 min.

9 Sprinkle the remaining flour over the
chicken and spoon over the cooked vegeta-
bles.
10 Mix together the wine and stock and pour
into the dish. Add the bouquet garni and the
bay leaves.
11 Cook, covered, on combination 250°/
microwave medium for 12 min.
12 Remove the bouquet garni and bay leaves
and stir in the cream.

Chicken pepperoni

1 medium green pepper
1 medium red pepper
225g (8oz) onion, chopped
4 tablespoons cooking oil
1 garlic clove, crushed
4×175g (7oz) chicken joints, skinned
salt and pepper
50g (2oz) cooked lean ham, chopped
400g (14oz) tin chopped tomatoes
1 bay leaf
1 pinch dried thyme
2 tablespoons cornflour
4 tablespoons red vermouth

1 Core and seed the peppers and slice thinly.
2 Place the peppers and onion in a bowl and
stir in 3 tablespoons oil. Sprinkle with the
crushed garlic.
3 Cook, uncovered, on microwave high for 4
min.
4 Brush the chicken joints with 1 tablespoon
oil and season with salt and pepper.
5 Place the chicken joints in a casserole and
add the cooked onion and pepper mixture.
6 Cook, uncovered, on combination 250°/
microwave medium for 10 min.
7 Stir in the ham, tomatoes, bay leaf and
thyme.
8 Cook, uncovered, on combination 250°/
microwave medium for 10 min.
9 Blend the cornflour with the vermouth and
gradually stir into the chicken.
10 Cook on microwave high for 3 min.
11 Remove the bay leaf and serve.

Stuffed chicken breast mornay

4×225g (8oz) chicken breasts, boned and
  skinned
150ml (¼pt) thick cheese sauce (see page 58)
100g (4oz) cooked ham, sliced
100g (4oz) mushrooms, thinly sliced
3 spring onions, chopped
salt and pepper

1 Use a sharp knife to cut a cavity in each
  chicken breast.
2 Place 1 tablespoon of cheese sauce in each
  cavity.
3 Divide the ham into 4 portions and stuff into
  each cavity.
4 Lightly grease a 22.5cm (9in) round Pyrex
  dish of 2.5 litre (3pt) capacity.
5 Mix together the mushrooms and spring
  onions and use half the quantity to form a
  layer in the dish.
6 Arrange the stuffed chicken breasts on top
  and season with salt and pepper.
7 Sprinkle the remainder of the vegetables
  over the chicken breasts.
8 Pour the remainder of the cheese sauce over
  the vegetables.
9 Pre-heat the oven on convection 250° for 5
  min.
10 Cook, uncovered, on combination 250°/
  microwave medium for 20 min.

Note: *If the cheese sauce has become too thick to
pour at stage 8, stir in 2 tablespoons milk and heat on
microwave high for 1 min.*

Chicken parcels

225g (8oz) sage and onion stuffing mix
350g (12oz) puff pastry
4×175g (7oz) chicken breasts, boned and
  skinned
salt and pepper
1 egg, lightly beaten

1 Mix the sage and onion stuffing as directed
  on the packet but slightly moister by adding
  a little extra water.
2 Roll pastry into four even shapes approx.
  15cm (6in) square.
3 Place a chicken breast diagonally on each
  square.
4 Divide the stuffing equally and spread on
  top the chicken breasts.
5 Season with salt and pepper.
6 Moisten the edges of the pastry with water
  and fold into triangular shapes. Seal the
  edges.
7 Brush with beaten egg.
8 Arrange the parcels around the edge of a
  lightly greased pizza tray with the apex of
  the triangle pointing in.
9 Chill in the refrigerator for 30 min.
10 Pre-heat the oven on convection 250° for 5
  min.
11 Place the chilled tray on the rack in the oven
  and cook on combination 250°/microwave
  medium for 16 min.

Chicken Parcels (above); Scalloped Potatoes (page 28)

Vegetables

Vegetables which have been correctly cooked in a microwave oven look and taste fresher than when prepared by any other method. This is because very little water is used and the vegetables cook largely in their own juices. This also means that more colour and goodness remain in the food rather than being poured down the sink. Small quantities are cooked much faster than by traditional methods and it is easy to prepare and cook a variety of vegetables one after the other. Reheating when required, either on a plate or in a serving dish is very fast with no drying out or spoiling.

Hints for perfectly cooked vegetables

1. Always cover vegetables during cooking. This will prevent loss of moisture and reduce the cooking time.

2. Salt can be used provided it is diluted in the water and not sprinkled directly onto the vegetables since this would cause dehydration.

3. More even cooking will result if a flat wide dish is used so that the vegetables are in even layers rather than heaped up.

4. Best results are obtained with small quantities especially for potatoes, carrots and other root vegetables. If a large quantity of potatoes is required it is better to cook in batches of 900g (2lb).

5. Stirring, half way through the cooking cycle, will ensure even results.

6. It is important that the vegetables on top are moist before cooking and this can be achieved by tossing the water over the vegetables in the dish.

7. The cooking times given in the recipes will have to be adjusted to suit personal preferences for crispness. Remember that food will continue to cook after the oven has been switched off.

8. For quantities up to 450g (1lb) use a 1200ml (2pt) casserole with lid and for quantities up to 900g (2lb) use a 2400ml (4pt) casserole with lid.

Basic instructions for cooking 450g (1lb) of fresh vegetables

Broccoli, Calabrese, Cauliflower: Cut into florets and add to a dish containing 1.25cm (½in) salted water. Toss the water over the vegetables and cook, covered, on microwave high for 8 min. Stir once during cooking.

Brussels sprouts: Prepare by trimming away loose leaves and cutting across the stalk end. Add 1.25cm (½in) salted water to a casserole. Add the sprouts and toss in the water. Cook, covered, on microwave high for 8 min.

Cabbage: Shred the cabbage and add to a casserole containing 1.25cm (½in) salted water. Toss the water over the surface of the cabbage and cook, covered, for 8 min. It is ESSENTIAL to move the layers of cabbage from the bottom to the top of the casserole at least twice during cooking.

Celery: Trim the stalks and cut into 2.5cm (1in) pieces. Add the celery to a dish containing 1.25cm (½in) salted water, Toss the water over the celery and cook, covered, on microwave high for 7 min.

Courgettes: Cut into slices and sprinkle with salt. Leave for 15 min and dry with kitchen towel. Season with black pepper and dot with butter. Cook, covered, on microwave high for 3 min. If preferred, 1 tablespoon of water can be substituted for the butter.

Leeks: Cut into 2.5cm (1in) pieces and place in a bowl with 15g (½oz) butter. Cook, covered, on microwave high for 3–4 min. Season to taste with salt and pepper. If preferred, 1 tablespoon of water can be substituted for the butter.

Onions: Chop into small pieces and place in a dish containing 1.25cm (½in) salted water. Cook, covered, on microwave high for 5–6 min.

Root vegetables – carrots, parsnips, potatoes, turnips: Cut the prepared vegetables into even sized pieces and place in a dish containing 1.25cm (½in) salted water. Toss the water over the vegetables and cook, covered, on microwave high for 10–12 min. Stir once during cooking.

Runner beans: Slice the prepared beans and place in a dish containing 1.25cm (½in) salted water. Toss the water over the beans and cook, covered, on microwave high for 10–12 min. Stir once during cooking.

Stuffed peppers

4 large green peppers
1 small onion, chopped
3 tablespoons finely chopped celery
15g (½oz) butter
225g (8oz) cooked ham, chopped
1 egg
1 tablespoon chopped parsley
salt and pepper

1 Cut the stalk ends off the peppers to give an opening for the stuffing.
2 Remove the core and seeds. Turn the peppers upside down and tap gently to remove any stray seeds.
3 Trim the flesh from around the stalks and chop into small pieces.
4 Combine the chopped flesh from the stalks with the onion, celery and butter in a bowl.
5 Cook, covered on microwave high for 5 min.
6 Drain off any liquid.
7 Add the ham, egg, parsley and seasoning and stir well.
8 Place the peppers, upright, on a rectangular flan dish and spoon in the stuffing evenly between the four.
9 Cook, uncovered, on microwave high for 7 min.

Note: *Any lean cooked meat can be substituted for the ham.*

Scalloped sweetcorn

Note: *For this recipe you will need two rectangular pie dishes. One to fit inside the other.*

350g (12oz) tin sweetcorn, juice retained
single cream or evaporated milk
100g (4oz) butter
2 tablespoons plain flour
salt and pepper
2 eggs, size 3, lightly beaten
2 tablespoons chopped red pepper
50g (2oz) fresh breadcrumbs
boiling water

1 Make up 300ml (½pt) liquid using the retained juice from the sweet corn and single cream or evaporated milk.
2 In a large jug melt 50g (2oz) butter on microwave high for 1 min.
3 Blend in the flour and gradually add the liquid, mixing until smooth.
4 Heat on microwave high for 30 sec and stir. Heat on microwave high for a further 30 sec and stir again.
5 Season with salt and pepper and blend in the beaten eggs, stirring continuously.
6 Stir in the peppers and sweetcorn.
7 Lightly grease the smaller of the two casseroles and pour in the mixture.
8 Melt the remaining 50g (2oz) butter in a bowl on microwave high for 1 min. Stir in the breadcrumbs and sprinkle over the sweetcorn mixture.
9 Pre-heat oven on convection 220° for 5 min.
10 Pour boiling water into the larger casserole and carefully place the smaller casserole into it so that the water level almost reaches the top.
11 Cook, uncovered, on combination 220°/ microwave medium for 10 min.

Stir-fry vegetables

2 spring onions, roughly chopped
1 small onion, chopped
1 medium potato
1 medium parsnip
¼ small swede
25g (1oz) butter
salt and pepper

1 Wash and peel the root vegetables and chop into small pieces.
2 Melt the butter in a casserole on microwave high for 1 min.
3 Add all the vegetables. Season with salt and pepper and stir well.
4 Cook, covered, on microwave high for 1 min. Stir well and cook for a further min on microwave high. Stir again and cook for 2 min on microwave high.

Note: *2 tablespoons vegetable oil can be substituted for the butter.*

Lancashire herb pot

1 medium onion, thinly sliced
3 large potatoes peeled and thinly sliced
4 lamb chops
1 tablespoon rosemary
225g (½lb) mushrooms, thinly sliced
400g (14oz) tin chopped tomatoes
25g (1oz) butter
salt and pepper

1 Place half of the onion in a layer in a lightly greased large rectangular casserole.
2 Make a second layer with half of the potatoes.
3 Place the lamb chops on top of the potatoes.
4 Sprinkle the rosemary over the chops.
5 Use the remaining onion to form the next layer.
6 Spread all of the mushrooms over the onion.
7 Pour on the tomatoes and spread evenly.
8 Make a top layer with the remaining potatoes, overlapping if necessary to give an attractive finish.
9 Cut the butter into small pieces and dot over the potatoes.
10 Season with salt and pepper.
11 Cook, uncovered on combination 250°/ microwave medium for 30 min.

Cauliflower cheese

1 medium cauliflower
300ml (½pt) thick cheese sauce (see page 58)
25g (1oz) grated cheese

1 Wash the cauliflower and separate into florets.
2 Place the cauliflower florets in a casserole containing 1.25cm (½in) salted water. Toss the water over the florets.
3 Cook, covered, on microwave high for 7 min or until the florets are just cooked. Stir once during cooking.
4 Drain the cauliflower and arrange stalks down in a pie dish.
5 Pour the cheese sauce over the cauliflower and sprinkle with the grated cheese.
6 Cook on convection 250° until the top is bubbling and golden brown.

Ratatouille

225g (8oz) courgettes, sliced
2 large aubergines, sliced
2 medium onions, sliced
1 clove garlic, crushed
3 tablespoons vegetable oil
3 large ripe tomatoes, skinned and chopped
1 green pepper, seeded and chopped
1 red pepper, seeded and chopped
1 tablespoon mixed herbs
salt and pepper

1 Soak the aubergines and courgettes in cold water for 30 min.
2 Place the onions, garlic and oil in a casserole.
3 Cook, uncovered, on microwave high for 5 min.
4 Drain the courgettes and aubergines and add, with the tomatoes and peppers to the dish. Stir well.
5 Cook, covered, on microwave high for 5 min.
6 Stir in the herbs and seasoning and cook, covered, on microwave high for a further 8 min.

Mushroom mediterranean

225g (8oz) button mushrooms, left whole
4 tablespoons chopped mixed red and green peppers
2 medium tomatoes, skinned and chopped
1 stick celery, chopped
1 small onion, chopped
1 tablespoon red wine
dash Worcester sauce
salt and pepper

1 Combine all the ingredients in a large casserole and stir well.
2 Cook, covered, on microwave high for 8 min. Stir once during cooking.

Serve as a vegetable with grilled steaks or chops.

VARIATION
Serve as a starter in individual dishes with grated cheese sprinkled on top. Melt the cheese on microwave high for 1 min per dish.

Quick Chilli Con Carne (page 14); Cauliflower Cheese (above)

Mushroom croquettes

150ml (¼pt) thick white sauce (see page 58)
½ teaspoon Worcester sauce
2 pinches curry powder
1 egg, size 3
12 cream cracker biscuits, crushed into crumbs
2 oz mushrooms, very finely chopped
½ teaspoon salt
½ teaspoon paprika

For the coating
1 egg, lightly beaten
golden breadcrumbs

1 Combine all the ingredients in a bowl and mix well.
2 Turn mixture out onto a floured board and roll into 3 cylindrical shapes 2.5cm (1in) in diameter.
3 Chill in a refrigerator for a minimum of 1½ hours.
4 When completely chilled cut each roll into 3; making 9 in all.
5 Roll each croquette in the beaten egg and then in the golden breadcrumbs until completely coated.
6 Pre-heat the oven on convection 250° for 5 min.
7 Place the croquettes on a well-greased pizza tray or flat dish and cook, uncovered, on combination 250°/microwave medium for 3 min. Turn the croquettes over and cook for a further 2 min.

Note: *The croquettes can be frozen after stage 5 until required.*

Scalloped potatoes

900g (2lb) potatoes, peeled, thinly sliced and washed
100g (4oz) onion, thinly sliced
50g (2oz) butter
salt and pepper
3 tablespoons plain flour
150ml (¼pt) milk
100g (4oz) grated cheese

1 Lightly grease a large deep Pyrex roasting dish.
2 Make a layer of sliced potatoes in the dish and sprinkle on some of the onion. Dot with butter and season with salt and pepper.
3 Continue to make layers of potato and onion, dotting with butter and seasoning and finishing with a layer of potato.
4 Mix the flour and milk into a smooth paste and gently pour over the potatoes.
5 Sprinkle the cheese evenly over.
6 Pre-heat the oven on convection 250° for 5 min.
7 Place the dish on a low rack in the oven and cook, uncovered, on combination 250°/microwave medium for 20 min or until the cheese is golden brown.

Jacket potatoes

Large baking potatoes

1 Wash the potatoes thoroughly and dry with kitchen towel.
2 Pierce the skins in several places with a fork to prevent bursting.
3 Pre-heat the oven on convection 250° for 5 min.
4 Cook on the rack in the oven on combination 250°/microwave medium for 6–7 min for each potato.

Note: *The precise cooking time will be determined by the size of the potatoes and the number cooked.*

FILLINGS
The possibilities are many but here are a few of my favourites. In all cases add salt and pepper to taste.
Cheese and paprika with a little butter.
Baked beans with crumbled, crisped streaky bacon.
Corned beef and pickles mashed with a little butter.
Tinned salmon or tuna.
Chicken curry leftovers.

Pasta, rice and cereals

Using the the latest pastas and grains that do not require pre-soaking, it is easy to cook appetising dishes quickly. There are no pots to clean since the bowl used for cooking and serving are one and the same. There are endless variations and it is very simple to convert your own favourite recipes to microwave cooking. Here are are a few of my own to get you started.

Hints on cooking pasta and rice

1. Always use a very large bowl or casserole because the water tends to boil over.
2. It is much quicker to boil water in a kettle than to use the microwave.
3. After adding the pasta or rice to the water, bring back to the boil in the microwave before starting to time the cooking process.
4. Salt should be dissolved in the boiling water before adding the pasta or rice.
5. It is not necessary to stir during cooking.
6. Add 1 tablespoon of oil to the boiling water to prevent pasta sticking.

Tagliatelle parmesan

100g (4oz) tagliatelle
600ml (1pt) boiling, salted water
1 tablespoon oil
2 tablespoons double cream
2 tablespoons parmesan cheese, grated
freshly ground black pepper

1 Stir tagliatelle and oil into boiling, salted water in a large bowl.
2 Cover the dish and using microwave high bring back to the boil and cook for 4 min.
3 Drain well and stir in double cream and grated parmesan cheese.
4 Season with freshly ground black pepper.
5 Serve at once.

VARIATION
For a quick, tasty sauce make cheese sauce (see page 57) and add 50g (2oz) tuna fish, 2 tablespoons cooked peas and 1 tablespoon sweetcorn kernels.

Wholemeal gnocci with cream cheese sauce

100g (4oz) wholemeal gnocci
600ml (1pt) boiling, salted water
1 tablespoon oil
3 tablespoons cream cheese
3 tablespoons milk
salt and pepper
1 dessertspoon tomato puree
1 tablespoon chives, chopped

1 Stir gnocci and oil into boiling, salted water in a large bowl.
2 Cover the dish and using microwave high bring back to the boil and cook for 9 min.
3 Drain and place to one side, covered.
4 Combine the cream cheese with the milk and seasonings in a Pyrex jug.
5 Cook for on microwave high for 1 min.
6 Stir in the tomato puree and chopped chives and cook on microwave high for 2 min.
7 Pour sauce over gnocci and serve at once.

Savoury noodles

100g (4oz) tagliatelle or other ribbon noodles
600ml (1pt) boiling, salted water
1 tablespoon oil
300ml (½pt) cheese sauce (see page 57)
50g (2oz) thickly sliced cooked ham, diced
1 spring onion, chopped
1 tablespoon mushrooms, chopped
1 tablespoon mixed peppers, chopped

1 Stir noodles and oil into boiling, salted water in a large bowl.
2 Cover the dish and using microwave high bring back to the boil and cook for 4 min.
3 Drain and keep to one side, covered.
4 Combine the remaining ingredients with the cheese sauce in a large Pyrex jug.
5 Cook on microwave high, uncovered, for 2 min or until hot.
6 Pour the sauce over the noodles and stir very gently until all the noodles are coated in the sauce.
7 Serve at once.

Ruotine

100g (4oz) ruotine
600ml (1pt) boiling, salted water
1 tablespoon oil

1 Stir ruotine and oil into boiling, salted water in a large bowl.
2 Cover the dish and using microwave high bring back to the boil and cook for 7 min.
3 Drain and serve.

Lasagne

6 leaves lasagne
900ml (1½pt) boiling, salted water
1 tablespoon oil
25g (1oz) cornflour
600ml (1pt) milk
50g (2oz) cheese, grated
675g (1½lb) lean minced beef
1 medium onion, chopped
1 medium tin tomatoes, roughly chopped, juice retained
1 beef stock cube
2 dessertspoons gravy granules
salt and pepper
paprika powder
grated cheese for topping

1 Place the lasagne leaves in a large deep dish and add the boiling salted water and oil.
2 Cook on microwave high, uncovered, for 11 min. submersing the leaves at least three times during cooking with a wooden spoon.
3 Drain and leave to one side.
4 Mix the cornflour with a little milk in a large Pyrex jug.
5 Gradually add the remainder of the milk, stirring to a smooth paste.
6 Stir in the grated cheese.
7 Cook on microwave high for 5 min. Stir every minute.
8 Leave the cheese sauce to one side.
9 Place the minced beef and chopped onion in a casserole and cook, uncovered, on microwave high for 6 min.

10 Drain off any surplus fat.
11 Add the chopped tomatoes and juices, crumbled beef stock cube and gravy granules. Season with salt, pepper and paprika. Stir well.
12 Cook, covered, on microwave high for 15 min.
13 Remove half the meat sauce from the casserole and reserve.
14 Make a layer with 3 lasagne leaves on top of the meat sauce in the casserole.
15 Pour on two-thirds of the cheese sauce.
16 Pour on the remainder of the meat sauce.
17 Make a final layer with the three remaining lasagne leaves.
18 Pour over the remaining cheese sauce and sprinkle with grated cheese.
19 Pre-heat the oven on convection 250° for 5 min.
20 Place the dish on the rack in the oven and cook on combination 250°/ microwave medium for 10 min. If a more brown look is wanted cook on convection 250° for a further 8 min or until satisfactory.

Spaghetti

100g (4oz) spaghetti
600ml (1pt) boiling, salted water

1 Lower the spaghetti into the boiling, salted water in a large bowl.
2 On microwave high setting bring back to the boil and cook, uncovered, for 5–6 min.
3 Leave to stand, covered, for 5 min.
4 Drain and serve at once.

Note: *to make Spaghetti Bolognese; add 1 tablespoon tomato puree and 1 small tin of chopped tomatoes to the Basic Meat Sauce recipe on page 57. Pour over the cooked spaghetti and serve at once.*

Lasagne (above); Shepherd's Pie (page 14)

Macaroni cheese

225g (8oz) macaroni
1 litre (1¾pt) boiling, salted water
1 tablespoon oil
salt and pepper
600ml (1pt) cheese sauce (see page 57)
1 tablespoon grated cheese

1 Stir macaroni and oil into boiling, salted water in a large bowl.
2 Cover the dish and using microwave high setting bring back to the boil and cook for 8 min.
3 Drain and season to taste with salt and pepper.
4 Grease a pie dish with butter.
5 Place the macaroni into the greased dish.
6 Make the cheese sauce and pour over the macaroni.
7 Sprinkle with grated cheese.
8 Pre-heat the oven on convection 250° for 5 min.
9 Cook on combination 250°/microwave medium for 10 min or until cheese is nicely browned.

Beef curry

800g (1¾lb) lean stewing steak, cubed
1 large onion, chopped
200g (½lb) whole button mushrooms
3 large carrots, chopped
3 tablespoons tomato puree
1 medium cooking apple, peeled, cored and sliced
2 dessertspoons sweet pickle
4 heaped teaspoons curry powder
1 teaspoon garlic salt
salt and pepper
600ml (1pt) hot beef stock

1 Combine all the ingredients in a large casserole.
2 Stir well and cover.
3 Cook on microwave high for 15 min.
4 Stir well and cook on microwave low/simmer for 1 hour 15 min.
5 If a thicker consistency is required, blend 1 teaspoon cornflour with a little water and stir into the cooked curry.
6 Serve with cooked rice.

Note: *Sliced bananas, salted peanuts, sliced tomatoes, shredded coconut, and sweet chutney served in separate dishes are colourful and tasty additions.*

Traditional rice pudding

75g (3oz) pudding rice
3 tablespoons sugar
600ml (1pt) fresh milk or 1 tin evaporated milk made up to 1pt
15g (½oz) butter

1 Grease a pie dish with butter.
2 Place the rice and sugar in the dish.
3 Pour on the milk.
4 Gently mix ingredients.
5 Dot with butter.
6 Pre-heat the oven on convection 250° for 5 min.
7 Place the dish on the rack in the oven and cook on combination 250°/microwave medium for 30 min. Stir at least twice during cooking.

Risotto milano

50g (2oz) butter
1 small onion, finely chopped
1 clove garlic, crushed
225g (8oz) long grain rice
600ml (1pt) chicken stock, very hot
generous pinch saffron
salt and pepper
pinch grated nutmeg
1 tablespoon tomato puree
parmesan cheese, grated

1 Place the butter, onion and garlic in a casserole and cook on microwave high for 2 min.
2 Gradually stir in the rice and keep stirring until every grain is separated.
3 Blend the saffron, salt, pepper, nutmeg and tomato puree into the hot chicken stock.

4 Pour the blended stock over the rice and stir well.
5 Cover and cook on microwave high for 18 min or until the rice is cooked.
6 Sprinkle with parmesan cheese.
7 Serve at once.

Note: *To give variety, add any combination of sliced mushrooms, chopped mixed peppers, sweetcorn, diced ham and shelled prawns after stage 5.*

Porridge *(serves 1)*

50g (2oz) quick porridge oats
240ml (8fl oz) milk or milk and water
pinch of salt

1 Mix porridge with salt and liquid in a Pyrex jug.
2 Cook on microwave high for 2 min or until porridge is to the required consistency.
3 Add extra salt or sugar to taste.
4 Serve immediately with milk or cream.

Savoury rice salad

225g (8oz) patna rice
600ml (1pt) boiling, salted water
25g (1oz) peeled prawns
2 tablespoons defrosted frozen peas
1 tablespoon mixed peppers, chopped
1 tablespoon sweetcorn
salt and pepper

1 Stir the rice into boiling, salted water in a large bowl.
2 Cover and cook on microwave high for 15 min or until the water is absorbed.
3 Rinse with cold water to remove excess starch and drain.
4 Allow rice to cool before adding remaining ingredients.
5 Stir gently and season to taste.

VARIATION
Curried rice. Cook the rice as directed for savoury rice adding 1 teaspoon of curry powder to the boiling water. Add 25g (1oz) raisins after rinsing the rice. Serve chilled.

Eggs and cheese

The recipes I have chosen are versatile enough to use as snacks, starters or main courses. They are quick to prepare and cook as well as being nutritious and inexpensive. Once you get the hang of it you will be able to convert your own egg and cheese recipes. It is only too easy to overcook eggs in the microwave oven so under-cook to begin with and then keep a watchful eye during the final cooking period. Do not attempt to boil eggs on microwave otherwise the shells will explode and make a dreadful mess inside your oven.

Poached eggs

1 tablespoon cold water
1 egg, size 3

1 Spoon the water into a small ramekin.
2 Heat on microwave high for 30 sec.
3 Break the egg into the hot water. Pierce the yolk and white once, with a skewer.
4 Cook on microwave high for 30 sec.
(The cooking time may vary by 10 sec either way depending upon the freshness of the egg.)

Note: *½ teaspoon butter may be substituted for the cold water, if preferred.*

Savoury quiche

225g (8oz) self-raising flour
pinch salt
50g (2oz) lard
50g (2oz) margarine
cold water
150g (6oz) unsmoked bacon
50g (2oz) mushrooms, sliced
4 eggs, size 3
300ml (½pt) single cream
1 tablespoon milk
150g (6oz) cheddar cheese, grated
salt and pepper
1 tomato, thinly sliced

1 Place the flour and salt in a large mixing bowl.
2 Cut the lard and margarine into cubes and rub into the flour until the mixture resembles breadcrumbs.
3 Mix in sufficient water to form a stiff dough.
4 Roll out the dough to line a lightly greased 20cm (8in) flan dish.
5 Lightly prick all over the base with a fork.
6 Separate 1 egg retaining yolk and white.
7 Brush the dough with the separated egg white.
8 Remove the rind and cut the bacon into small pieces.
9 Lightly, beat the 3 eggs and the reserved yolk and stir in the cream, milk and grated cheese. Season with salt and pepper.
10 Arrange the sliced mushrooms and bacon pieces in the flan case and pour over the egg mixture.
11 Decorate with the tomato slices.
12 Place the dish on the rack in the oven and cook on combination 250°/microwave medium for 20 min.

Savoury creamed eggs

6 eggs, size 3, lightly beaten
6 tablespoons double cream
100g (4oz) cheddar cheese, grated
salt and pepper
15g (½oz) butter
1 extra tablespoon grated cheese
900ml (1½pt) boiling water

1 Combine the beaten eggs, double cream and grated cheese. Season with salt and pepper.
2 Grease a 600ml (1pt) oval pie dish with the butter.
3 Pour in egg mixture.
4 Sprinkle with the extra grated cheese.
5 Pour the boiling water into a 1½ litre (2pt) oval pie dish and place the smaller dish into the larger one. Ensure that the water level is over the level of the egg mixture.
6 Pre-heat oven on convection 250° for 5 min.
7 Place the dish on the rack in the oven and cook, uncovered, on combination 250°/microwave medium for 9 min or until the cheese is melted and bubbling.

Savoury Quiche (above); Savoury Rice Salad (page 33)

Scrambled eggs

2 eggs, size 3
knob of butter
2 tablespoons milk
salt and pepper

1 Break the eggs into a 600ml (1pt) Pyrex jug.
2 Whisk in the butter, milk and seasoning.
3 Cook, uncovered, on microwave high for 1 min.
4 Stir well and cook on microwave high for 1½ min or until the mixture rises and thickens. Do not overcook. Stir well and serve immediately.

Ham and egg surprise

6 hard boiled eggs, cooled, shelled and cut in halves
50g (2oz) fresh breadcrumbs
1 tablespoon milk
150g (6oz) minced ham
25g (1oz) onion, finely chopped
25g (1oz) mushrooms, finely chopped
1 teaspoon mustard powder
1 egg, beaten
1 pinch pepper

1 Arrange the boiled eggs, yolk side down, in a lightly greased 600ml (1pt) rectangular pie dish.
2 Combine all the other ingredients in a bowl. Mix well.
3 Cover the eggs with the mixture and level the surface.
4 Pre-heat the oven on convection 250° for 5 min.
5 Place the dish on the rack in the oven and cook, uncovered, on convection 250° for 20 min or until the top is browned and crisp. Serve cold, as a lunch or supper dish for two, or as a starter for four.

Note: *The laborious mincing and chopping can be avoided by the use of a food processor. All the ingredients for the topping may be processed together.*

Cheesy pork bake

100g (4oz) mushrooms, sliced
3 spring onions, chopped
4 pork chops
salt and pepper
300ml (½pt) thick cheese sauce (see page 58)
25g (1oz) cheese, grated
7 rashers streaky bacon

1 Place half of the mushrooms and spring onions in a lightly greased 22.5cm (9in) Pyrex dish of 2 litre (3pt) capacity.
2 Place the pork chops on top. Season lightly.
3 Pour the cheese sauce over the chops.
4 Sprinkle the remaining mushrooms and spring onions over. Season lightly.
5 Sprinkle with the grated cheese.
6 Cover with the bacon rashers.
7 Pre-heat the oven on convection 250° for 5 min.
8 Cook, uncovered, on combination 250°/microwave medium for 15 min.

Cheese and potato pie

900g (2lb) mashed potatoes (to boil potatoes see page 24)
100g (4oz) cheddar cheese, grated
25g (1oz) butter
1 tablespoon double cream
salt and pepper
1 tomato, thinly sliced
1 tablespoon grated cheese

1 Mix together the potatoes, grated cheese, butter and cream. Season with salt and pepper.
2 Turn the mixture into a greased 1.1 litre (2pt) oval pie dish.
3 Level the surface and decorate with the tomato slices.
4 Sprinkle with the tablespoon of grated cheese.
5 Pre-heat on convection 250° for 5 min.
6 Place the dish on the rack in the oven and cook on convection 250° for 12 min or until the melted cheese turns golden brown.

Desserts

Thanks to your combination oven you can make exciting puddings as often as you want and not have to resort to tinned peaches and ice cream because of lack of time. Most of the recipes use ingredients entirely from the store cupboard and are simple and quick to prepare. If you are slimming I suggest that you do not read any further. Where pastry is specified, either completely defrosted frozen or freshly made can be used with equal success. All the recipes in this section are cooked uncovered and sponge mixtures must be watched during the final stages in the oven to prevent overcooking.

Peach sponge pudding

50g (2oz) margarine
50g (2oz) caster sugar
1 egg, size 3
1 tablespoon milk
50g (2oz) self-raising flour
6 tinned peach halves
150ml (¼pt) reserved peach syrup
50g (2oz) ground almonds
3 glacé cherries, halved
demerara sugar

1 Cream the margarine and caster sugar until light and fluffy.
2 Add the egg and mix in the milk and flour.
3 Turn the mixture into a greased, 17.5cm (7in) round Pyrex sponge dish.
4 Cook on microwave high for 2 min.
5 Remove the sponge and pre-heat the oven on convection 250° for 5 min.
6 Mix the peach syrup with the ground almonds and stir until smooth.
7 Prick the sponge base all over with a fork.
8 Place the peaches, cut side down, in the sponge and pour over the almond syrup.
9 Top each peach with half a glacé cherry and sprinkle with demerara sugar.
10 Cook on combination 250°/microwave medium for 4 min.
11 Chill well before serving.

Steamed sponge pudding

100g (4oz) soft margarine
100g (4oz) caster sugar
2 eggs, size 3
100 g (4oz) self-raising flour
4 tablespoons milk
3 tablespoons jam

1 Cream the margarine and sugar until light and fluffy.
2 Add the eggs and fold in the flour. Gradually add the milk and stir until smooth.
3 Spoon the jam into a lightly greased 1.1 litre (2pt) pudding basin.
4 Pour the mixture on top.
5 Cook, uncovered, on microwave high for 5 min.

ALTERNATIVE
Substitute golden syrup or marmalade for the jam.

Mock meringue pavlova

275g (10oz) icing sugar
1 egg white, size 3

1 Mix icing sugar and egg white to form a stiff fondant.
2 Divide the mixture into 2 portions.
3 Roll out each portion to make a 15cm (6in) circle using icing sugar on a board to prevent sticking.
4 Trim a circlet of greaseproof paper to the size of the oven turntable.
5 Place one of the fondant circles on the paper and cook on microwave high for 2 min. Repeat with the second fondant.
6 Sandwich together, with a filling of fruit and ice-cream, fresh strawberries and strawberry syrup or hazelnuts and honey. Serve immediately.

Important: *Unlike conventionally baked meringue the structure of microwave meringue is quickly dissolved. Filling and decoration with piped cream should be left until just before serving.*

37

Sweet mincemeat parcels

375g (13oz) puff pastry
1 jar sweet mincemeat
milk
caster sugar

1 Divide the pastry into 4 equal pieces.
2 Roll out each piece, on a floured surface, to a 15cm (6in) square.
3 Divide the mincemeat evenly between the four squares, spreading diagonally so that the pastry can be folded into a triangle.
4 Dampen the edges of each square with milk and fold into triangular shapes.
5 Make 3 slits in the top of each parcel.
6 Brush each triangle with milk and dust with caster sugar.
7 Arrange each triangle, pointed side to the centre, on a greased pizza tray.
8 Pre-heat the oven on convection 250° for 5 min.
9 Cook on combination 250°/microwave medium for 11 minutes or until golden brown.

VARIATION
The parcels may be filled with thinly sliced apples or pears, topped with honey or with lightly stewed apricots sprinkled with ground almonds.

Lemon syllabub

½ tablet lemon jelly
150ml (¼pt) cold water
150ml (¼pt) whipping cream
1 tablespoon brandy
grated rind of 1 lemon
1 tablespoon lemon juice

1 Place the jelly in a jug and heat on microwave high for 30 sec, or until melted.
2 Mix in the cold water and leave to cool.
3 Whip the cream in a bowl until thickened.
4 When the jelly is almost set pour into the cream and add the other ingredients. Mix well.
5 Serve chilled in individual glasses.

Custard

2 tablespoons custard powder
2 tablespoons sugar
600ml (1pt) milk

1 In a 1.1 litre (2pt) jug, mix the custard powder and sugar with some of the milk to a smooth paste.
2 Gradually stir in the remainder of the milk and mix thoroughly.
3 Cook on microwave high for 5-6 min.
4 Stir once during cooking.
5 Taste and add additional sugar if required.

Old English apple dumplings

4 medium cooking apples
plain flour
375g (13oz) short crust pastry
demerara sugar
milk
granulated sugar

1 Peel and core the apples. With a sharp knife make a score around the centre of each apple.
2 Dust each apple with plain flour.
3 Divide the pastry into 4 equal portions.
4 On a floured surface, roll out each portion to make a circle large enough to completely wrap an apple.
5 Place an apple in the centre of each pastry circle and fill the core with demerara sugar.
6 Moisten the edge of each circle with milk and wrap neatly around the apples.
7 Place the dumpling, sealed end down, on buttered shallow flan dish.
8 Using the point of knife, gently pierce the pastry over the filling.
9 Brush with milk and sprinkle with granulated sugar.
10 Pre-heat the oven on combination 250° for 5 min.
11 Place the dish on the rack in the oven and cook on combination 250°/microwave medium for 14 min or until the pastry is golden brown.

Old English Apple Dumplings (above); Rhubarb Crisp (page 61)

Chocolate pear pudding

100g (4oz) soft margarine
100g (4oz) caster sugar
2 eggs, size 3
75g (3oz) self raising flour
25g (1oz) cocoa powder
2 tablespoons milk
1×800g (1lb 12oz) tin pear halves, drained
1 chocolate flake, crumbled
1 glacé cherry

1 Cream the margarine and sugar until light and fluffy.
2 Mix in the eggs, one at a time, with a little of the flour.
3 Add the cocoa powder and the remainder of the flour. Gradually, stir in the milk and mix until smooth.
4 Arrange the pear halves, cut side up, in a lightly greased 17.5cm (7in) cake dish.
5 Pour the chocolate mixture over the pears and level the surface.
6 Cook, on microwave high for 6 min.
7 Leave to cool for 5 min before turning out onto a serving plate.
8 Sprinkle with crumbled chocolate flake and decorate with the cherry in the centre. Serve immediately.

Lemon meringue pie

225g (8oz) short crust pastry
1 packet lemon meringue pie mix
1 egg, size 3
50g (2oz) caster sugar

1 On a floured surface, roll out the pastry large enough to line a 20cm (8in) Pyrex sponge dish.
2 Grease the dish and line with the pastry. Trim the edge and gently pierce the base all over with a fork.
3 Line with greaseproof paper and fill with dried beans or rice.
4 Pre-heat the oven on convection 250° for 5 min.
5 Place the dish on the rack in the oven and cook on combination 250°/microwave medium for 5 min.

6 Remove from the oven; remove the beans and greaseproof paper and set aside to cool.
7 Separate the egg, reserving the white and yolk.
8 Pour into a jug the contents of the pie mix packet. Make as instructed and stir in the egg yolk.
9 Cook on microwave high for 3 min or until the mixture thickens and the lemon capsule has dissolved.
10 Whisk the egg white until standing in peaks.
11 Gently fold in the caster sugar.
12 Pour the lemon pie filling into the pastry case and spread the meringue mixture completely over the surface.
13 Cook on convection 220° until the meringue is golden brown.

ALTERNATIVE
Make fresh lemon curd (see page 54) and substitute for the pie mix to give a richer pudding. As an alternative to lemon, fill the flan with stewed apples, rhubarb or apricots. For something really different make a butterscotch sauce (page 58) and add the egg yolk.

Egg custard

150ml (¾pt) milk
3 eggs, size 3
1 tablespoon granulated sugar
boiling water
grated nutmeg

1 Heat the milk, in a jug, on microwave high for 3 min.
2 Whisk the eggs and sugar in a 600ml (1pt) oval pie dish.
3 Pour in the heated milk and stir well.
4 Place the dish containing the custard into another dish, slightly larger but the same shape, containing boiling water. The level of the water must reach the level of the custard in the smaller dish.
5 Cook on microwave high for 5 min.
6 Remove the dish of custard from the boiling water and leave to stand for 5 min.
7 Sprinkle with grated nutmeg and serve.

Strawberry affairé

13oz puff pastry
1 egg, size 3, beaten
300ml (½pt) whipping cream
225g (8oz) fresh strawberries
caster sugar
strawberry jam

1 Divide the pastry equally and roll out 2 rec-
tangles approx. 25×17.5cm (10×7in) on a
floured surface.
2 Brush the tops with the beaten egg.
3 Pre-heat the oven on convection 250° for 5
min.
4 Cover the rack in the oven with a circlet of
greaseproof paper. Place one pastry on the
paper and cook on combination 250°/
microwave medium for 6 min or until
golden brown. Remove from the oven and
repeat with the second pastry.
5 Allow the puff pastries to cool.
6 Meanwhile, whip the cream to piping con-
sistency.
7 Hull and wash the strawberries and toss in
caster sugar.
8 Spread each cooled pastry with strawberry
jam.
9 Pipe the cream on top and decorate with the
strawberries.
10 Place one on top of the other on a serving
plate.

(See colour photograph on front cover)

Traditional Christmas pudding

125g (5oz) plain flour
3 tablespoons mixed spice
50g (2oz) nuts, chopped
150g (6oz) fresh breadcrumbs
225g (8oz) soft brown sugar
225g (8oz) shredded suet
600g (1lb 6oz) mixed dried fruit
50g (2oz) glacé cherries
1 medium eating apple, peeled and grated
grated rind of 1 lemon
4 eggs, size 3
3 tablespoons black treacle
2 tablespoons milk or stout

1 Thoroughly mix all of the ingredients in a
large bowl.
2 Lightly grease 3×600ml (1pt) pudding
basins.
3 Divide the mixture between the bowls and
cover with plastic wrap.
4 Cook, one at a time, on microwave high for 5
min.

Note: *The same quantity makes 2×900ml (1½pt)
puddings and are cooked on microwave high for 8
min each.*

It is not recommended that the puddings be
kept for more than 7 days before using. How-
ever, they may be cooked in advance and stored
in the deep freeze.

Jam roly-poly

225g (8oz) self-raising flour
100g (4oz) shredded suet
cold water
jam
milk
1 tablespoon caster sugar
½ teaspoon ground cinnamon

1 Mix the flour and suet with enough water to
form a soft dough.
2 On a floured surface, roll the dough into an
oblong shape 1.25cm (½in) thick.
3 Spread one side with jam leaving a 1.25cm
(½in) border.
4 Brush the border with milk and roll up from
the narrow end and seal the edges.
5 Place the roly-poly on a trimmed sheet of
buttered greaseproof paper. Roll up loosely
and secure the ends with elastic bands.
6 Wrap in plastic wrap.
7 Place on the turntable in the oven and cook
on microwave high for 8 min.
8 Carefully unwrap the roly-poly and place on
a serving plate.
9 Sprinkle with a mixture of caster sugar and
ground cinnamon.

Old-fashioned bread pudding

225g (8oz) mixed dry fruit
50g (2oz) butter
225g (8oz) stale bread
2 eggs, size 3
300ml (½pt) milk
50g (2oz) granulated sugar
½ teaspoon salt
1 teaspoon vanilla essence
¼ teaspoon grated nutmeg
1 teaspoon mixed spice
demerara sugar

1 Combine the fruit with the butter in a bowl and heat on microwave high for 2 min.
2 Tear the bread into very small pieces in a large bowl.
3 Mix the eggs with the milk and pour over the bread.
4 Add the heated fruit and all the other ingredients, except the demerara sugar. Mix well together.
5 Turn the mixture into a well-buttered ring mould. Level the top neatly and sprinkle liberally with demerara sugar.
6 Pre-heat the oven on convection 250° for 5 min.
7 Place on the rack in the oven and cook on combination 250°/microwave medium for 11 min.
8 Allow to cool before turning out on serving plate.

Bread and butter pudding

600ml (1 pt) milk
4 large slices bread
butter
50g (2oz) mixed dried fruit
50g (2oz) demerara sugar
2 eggs, size 3

1 Heat the milk, in a large jug, on microwave high for 3 min.
2 Butter the bread generously, remove the crusts and cut into strips.
3 Grease a 1.1 litre (2pt) oval pie dish. Use half of the bread strips, buttered side up, to make a layer across the dish.
4 Sprinkle the dried fruit and 25g (1oz) of sugar over the bread.
5 Use the remaining bread strips, buttered side up, to make a further layer.
6 Beat the eggs into the warm milk and strain over the bread layers.
7 Sprinkle the remaining sugar over the top and allow to stand for 30 min.
8 Pre-heat the oven on convection 250° for 5 min.
9 Place the dish on the rack in the oven and cook on combination 250°/microwave medium for 10 min.

Bread pudding

225g (8oz) white bread, with crusts removed
240ml (8fl. oz) milk
50g (2oz) margarine
50g (2oz) dark brown sugar
1 egg, size 3, lightly beaten
225g (8oz) mixed dried fruit
2 teaspoons mixed spice

1 Tear the bread into small pieces in a large bowl.
2 Pour the milk over the bread and beat until smooth.
3 Melt the margarine in a bowl on microwave high for 1 min.
4 Add to the bread mixture along with all the other ingredients. Mix well.
5 Turn the mixture into a greased ring mould and smooth the surface.
6 Cook on microwave defrost for 10 min. Allow the dish to stand for 10 min inside the oven. Cook on microwave defrost for a further 10 min.
7 Allow to cool before turning out on a serving plate.

Note: *For a crisp top, sprinkle with demerara sugar and place under a hot grill for a few minutes.*

Fruit Scones (page 45); Rich Fruit Cake (page 48)

French jam slice

225g (8oz) puff pastry
75g (3oz) jam
milk
icing sugar

1 On a floured surface, roll out the pastry to a rectangle 22.5×17.5cm (9×7in).
2 Cut into 2 equal portions and put one aside. Spread the other with the jam leaving a 1.25cm (½in) border all round.
3 Moisten the edges with milk.
4 Place the reserved pastry portion on top of the jam covered one. Seal the edges and trim neatly.
5 Make 5cm (2in) slits about 2.5cm (1in) apart along the top and brush with milk.
6 Pre-heat the oven on convection 250° for 5 min.
7 Cover the rack in the oven with a circlet of greaseproof paper. Place the jam slice on the paper and cook on combination 250°/microwave medium for 8 min or until golden brown.
8 Dust with icing sugar and serve hot or cold.

Apple crumble

75g (3oz) soft margarine
150g (6oz) self-raising flour
75g (3oz) granulated sugar
350g (12oz) cooking apples, peeled and thinly sliced
2 tablespoons granulated sugar

1 Rub the margarine into the flour until soft crumbs are formed.
2 Stir in 75g (3oz) granulated sugar.
3 Place the sliced apples in a lightly greased 1.1 litre (2pt) oval pie dish.
4 Sprinkle with 2 tablespoons granulated sugar.
5 Sprinkle the crumble over the fruit and level the top.
6 Pre-heat the oven on convection 250° for 5 min.
7 Place the dish on the rack in the oven and cook on combination 250°/microwave medium for 10 min.

Cakes

The saying 'baking is a science whilst cooking is an art' may be true and the precise measuring of ingredients helps success but more total failures occur in microwave baking than any other use of the oven. Much of the fault lies with overcooking though there has been prejudice against microwave baked cakes because of the inability to get a browned appearance. No such problem should occur with cakes baked in a combination oven where you have the advantage of speed with a traditional finish. Do remember that you should only use traditional baking tins if the instructions with your oven allow it. The alternative is Pyrex dishes or plastic ones specially made for combination ovens.

Fruit scones

225g (8oz) plain flour
50g (2oz) caster sugar
pinch of salt
1 teaspoon bi-carbonate of soda
2 teaspoons cream of tartar
50g (2oz) soft margarine
75g (3oz) sultanas
5 tablespoons milk

1 Mix the flour, sugar, salt, bi-carbonate of soda cream of tartar together in a large bowl.
2 Rub in the margarine until crumbly.
3 Add the sultanas and milk and stir until a stiff dough is formed.
4 On a floured surface, roll out till 1.25cm (½in) thick.
5 Cut into rounds with a scone cutter.
6 Remove the turntable from the oven and pre-heat on convection 220° for 5 min.
7 Divide the scones into two batches and place on lightly greased pizza trays.
8 Place one tray on the rack in the oven and cook on convection 220° for 12 min. Repeat with the second batch of scones.

Cherry coconut cake

100g (4oz) margarine
100g (4oz) caster sugar
2 eggs, size 3
150g (6oz) self-raising flour
4 tablespoons desiccated coconut
4 tablespoons milk
50g (2oz) glacé cherries, halved and tossed in flour

1 Cream the margarine and sugar till light and fluffy.
2 Add the eggs, one at a time, with a little of the flour.
3 Stir in the remainder of the flour, coconut and milk. Mix well.
4 Gently stir in the cherries.
5 Turn into a lightly greased 450g (1lb) loaf dish and level the surface.
6 Pre-heat the oven on convection 250° for 5 min.
7 Place the rack in the oven and cook on combination 250°/combination medium for 9–10 min.
8 Leave to cool in the dish before turning out.

Gingerbread

50g (2oz) margarine
50g (2oz) soft brown sugar
2 tablespoons golden syrup
100g (4oz) self-raising flour
1 tablespoon ground ginger
1 egg, size 3
1 tablespoon milk

1 Place the margarine, sugar and syrup in a bowl.
2 Heat on microwave high for 2 min.
3 Mix thoroughly and add the flour and ground ginger.
4 Add the egg and milk and stir well.
5 Turn the mixture into a lightly-greased 450g (1lb) loaf dish and smooth the surface.
6 Cook on microwave high for 3 min or until the edges are starting to leave the sides of the dish. The cake should still be slightly moist on top.
7 Allow to cool before turning out.

Date and walnut teabread

225g (8oz) self-raising flour
150g (6oz) caster sugar
½ teaspoon salt
100g (4oz) lard
75g (3oz) dates, stoned and chopped
75g (3oz) walnut kernels, chopped
2 eggs, size 3, beaten

1 Combine the flour, sugar and salt in a large mixing bowl.
2 Rub in the lard until evenly textured.
3 Add the dates, walnuts and beaten eggs. Mix well.
4 Turn the mixture into a greased and floured 450g (1lb) loaf dish. Level the surface.
5 Pre-heat the oven on convection 220° for 5 min.
6 Cook, uncovered, on combination 220°/microwave medium for 10 min.

Note: *Margarine may be substituted for lard.*

Victoria sandwich

150g (6oz) soft margarine
150g (6oz) caster sugar
3 eggs, size 3
150g (6oz) self-raising flour
2 tablespoons milk
raspberry jam

1 Cream the margarine and sugar until light and fluffy.
2 Add the eggs, one at a time, with a little of the flour.
3 Gradually add the rest of the flour. Add the milk and mix well.
4 Divide the mixture between two 20cm (8in) lightly greased sandwich dishes and level the surface.
5 Pre-heat the oven on convection 250° for 5 min.
6 Separately, cook each half of the sandwich, uncovered, on combination 250°/microwave medium for 6 min each.
7 Allow to cool slightly before turning out.
8 When completely cool, spread one half with jam and sandwich together.

Battenburg cake

100g (4oz) caster sugar
100g (4oz) margarine
2 eggs, size 3
100g (4 oz) self-raising flour
1 tablespoon milk
red and yellow food colouring
raspberry jam
250g (9oz) block marzipan

1 Cream the sugar and margarine until light and fluffy.
2 Mix in the eggs, one at a time, with a little of the flour.
3 Gradually mix in the rest of the flour along with the milk.
4 Divide the mixture equally into two bowls.
5 Colour one half pale yellow and the other pink with a few drops of food colouring.
6 Turn the yellow mixture into a lightly greased 450g (1lb) loaf dish and level the top. Do the same with the pink mixture in another dish.
7 Cook each dish separately, uncovered, on microwave high for 2 min or until the top is only just cooked but still slightly moist.
8 Allow both dishes to cool before turning out.
9 Carefully slice each cake in half, lengthwise.
10 Spread with raspberry jam and sandwich the halves together, alternating the colours to give a chequered pattern.
11 Roll out the marzipan large enough to wrap once round the cake.
12 Spread jam over the top surface of the marzipan.
13 Place the cake in the centre of the marzipan and wrap round once.
14 Trim the ends to show the chequered pattern.
15 Completely wrap the cake in greaseproof paper.
16 Place in the refrigerator to chill before cutting.

Victoria Sandwich (above); Bread Pudding (page 42)

Light fruit cake

150g (6oz) margarine
225g (8oz) granulated sugar
3 eggs, size 3
225g (8oz) self-raising flour
150g (6oz) mixed dried fruit
3 tablespoons milk

1 Cream the margarine and sugar until light and fluffy.
2 Add the eggs, one at a time, with a little of the flour.
3 Heat the dried fruit, in a dish, on microwave high for 45 sec and add to the mixture.
4 Fold in the remainder of the flour and add the milk. Mix well.
5 Grease a 17.5cm (7in) Pyrex cake dish and line with greaseproof paper.
6 Turn the mixture into the prepared dish and level the surface.
7 Place the dish on the rack in the oven and cook on combination 250°/microwave medium for 12 min.

Note: *Butter may be substituted for margarine.*

Rich fruit cake

350g (12oz) mixed dried fruit
125g (5oz) glacé cherries, chopped
50g (2oz) mixed dried peel
50g (2oz) nuts, chopped
150g (6oz) soft brown sugar
juice of 1 lemon
½ medium carrot, grated
100g (4oz) soft margarine
1 teaspoon mixed spice
150ml (6floz) milk
350g (12oz) self-raising flour
2 eggs, size 3

1 Place the dried fruit, cherries, peel, nuts, sugar, lemon juice, grated carrot, margarine, spice and milk into a large mixing bowl.
2 Heat on microwave high for 10 min. Stir every 2 min.

3 Allow the mixture to cool at room temperature.
4 When cool, add the the flour and eggs. Mix well.
5 Grease a 17.5cm (7in) Pyrex cake dish and line with greaseproof paper.
6 Turn the mixture into the prepared dish and make a slight hollow in the centre.
7 Place the cake on the rack in the oven and cook on combination 220°/microwave medium for 17 min. Test with a skewer and, if the cake is cooked, it should be clean. If not ready, continue cooking but test every min.

Quickest-ever Christmas cake

100g (4oz) margarine
100g (4oz) soft brown sugar
2 eggs, size 3
1 tablespoon black treacle
50g (2oz) glacé cherries, chopped and rolled in flour
600g (1lb 6oz) mixed dried fruit
25g (1oz) nuts, chopped
grated rind ½ lemon
grated rind ½ orange
125g (5oz) plain flour
15g (½oz) cocoa powder
½ teaspoon mixed spice
2 tablespoons sherry

1 Cream the margarine and sugar until light and fluffy in a large mixing bowl.
2 Beat the eggs and treacle in a bowl and add to the mixture.
3 Add the cherries, dried fruit and nuts and mix well.
4 Stir in the remainder of the ingredients. Mix well.
5 Grease a 20cm (8in) Pyrex cake dish and line with greaseproof paper.
6 Turn the mixture into the prepared dish and level the surface.
7 Cook on microwave defrost for 38 min or until the cake is no longer wet on top.

Important: *Defrost setting is the lowest available.*
Note: *Milk may be substituted for sherry.*

Easy-bake Christmas cake

125g (5oz) soft margarine
125g (5oz) dark soft brown sugar
1 dessertspoon black treacle
4 eggs, size 3
125g (5oz) plain flour
15g (½oz) cocoa powder
½ teaspoon salt
1½ teaspoon mixed spice
2 tablespoons sherry
600g (1lb 6oz) mixed dried fruit
100g (4oz) glacé cherries, chopped and rolled in
   flour
50g (2oz) nuts, chopped
finely grated rind ½ lemon
finely grated rind ½ orange

1 Cream the margarine and sugar until light
   and fluffy.
2 Add the treacle and mix well.
3 Add the eggs, one at a time, with a little of
   the flour.
4 Sift the remainder of the flour, cocoa, salt
   and mixed spice gradually into the bowl.
   Stir in the sherry.
5 Add the dried fruit, cherries, nuts and grated
   peel. Mix well.
6 Grease a 20cm (8in) Pyrex cake dish and
   line with greaseproof paper.
7 Turn the mixture into the prepared dish and
   make a slight hollow in the centre.
8 Place the dish on the rack in the oven and
   cook on combination 160°/microwave
   medium for 12 min.
9 Cook on microwave defrost for a further 20
   min. Test with a skewer which should be
   clean if the cake is cooked.
10 Allow to slightly cool in the dish before
   turning out.

Lemon crisps

225g (8oz) plain flour
125g (5oz) butter
rind of 2 lemons, finely grated
125g (5oz) caster sugar
yellow food colouring
1 teaspoon lemon juice

1 Place the flour in a large mixing bowl and
   rub in the butter.
2 Add the lemon rind and half of the sugar.
3 Knead firmly and work in the remainder of
   the sugar.
4 Stir in a few drops of colouring and the
   lemon juice.
5 Divide into 2 portions.
6 Roll each portion into a cylindrical shape
   17.5cm (7in) long.
7 Wrap in greaseproof paper and refrigerate
   for a minimum of 3 hours.
8 Unwrap and cut each cylinder into 18 slices.
9 Lightly grease the oven turntable and pre-
   heat on convection 250° for 5 min.
10 Place 9 slices directly onto the turntable and
   cook on combination 250°/microwave
   medium for 6 min.
11 Repeat for each batch of 9 slices.

Note: *Remember to clean the turntable on comple-
tion.*

Bread and biscuits

Everyone agrees that home-baked is best and nothing is more tempting to the taste buds than the delicious aroma of freshly baked bread and biscuits. Even if you have never attempted to bake bread these recipes are so simple that you can be assured of perfect results – first and every time. If your oven specifically allows the use of metal dishes then you may use conventional loaf tins otherwise you must use special containers such as Pyrex which are suitable for use in a combination oven. If your combination oven has a full range of microwave settings considerable time can be saved by proving the dough on the lowest power. Allow approx 18 min for dough made with 900g (2lb) flour. An airing cupboard is a good alternative but it will take at least 2 hours for the same result.

Brown bread

300ml (½pt) milk
15g (½oz) fresh yeast
225g (8oz) wholemeal flour
225g (8oz) plain flour
1 teaspoon salt
15g (½oz) butter
2 teaspoons malt extract

1 Heat the milk in a 600ml (1pt) jug on microwave high for 2 min.
2 Mix the yeast with a little of the milk and leave to stand for 10 min.
3 Mix the flours and salt together in a large bowl and rub in the butter.
4 Mix the malt extract into the remainder of the milk. Gradually, add to the flour along with the yeast and mix to a smooth dough.
5 Turn out onto a floured surface and knead for 10 min or until smooth and elastic.
6 Transfer the dough to clean bowl and cover with a damp tea cloth. Leave in a warm place for 2 hours or until the dough has doubled in size.
7 Turn out onto a floured surface and knead for a few min.

8 Grease a 900g (2lb) loaf container and add the dough.
9 Sprinkle the top with flour and cover with oiled plastic wrap. Leave in a warm place for 30 min or until the dough has risen to the top of the container.
10 Remove the plastic wrap and place the container on the rack in the oven.
11 Cook, uncovered, on combination 250°/microwave medium for 13 min. Turn the loaf upside down in the dish and cook for a further 10 min.

White bread

300ml (½pt) milk.
15g (½oz) fresh yeast
450g (1lb) strong white bread flour
1 teaspoon salt
1 teaspoon cooking oil

1 Warm the milk in a 600ml (1pt) jug on microwave high for 2 min.
2 Mix the yeast with a little of the milk and leave to stand for 10 min.
3 Sift the flour and salt into a large mixing bowl.
4 Make a well in the centre of the flour and pour in the yeast mixture, the remainder of the milk and the cooking oil. Mix to a smooth dough.
5 Turn out the dough onto a floured surface and knead for 10 min or until the dough is smooth and elastic.
6 Transfer to a clean bowl and cover with a damp tea cloth. Leave in a warm place for 2 hours or until the dough has doubled in size.
7 Turn out onto a floured surface and knead for 3–4 min.
8 Grease a 900g (2lb) loaf container. Press in the dough and sprinkle the top with flour.
9 Cover with oiled plastic wrap and leave in a warm place for 30 min or until the dough has risen to the top of the container.
10 Remove the plastic wrap and place the container on the rack in the oven.
11 Cook, uncovered, on combination 250°/microwave medium for 13 min. Turn the loaf upside down in the dish and cook for a further 10 min.

Pizza (page 52); Ratatouille (page 26); Stuffed Peppers (page 25)

Pizza base

Use ¼ of the dough for white or brown bread (see page 50) for each pizza base.

1 On a floured surface, roll out the dough to a circle approximately 20cm (8in) in diameter.
2 Transfer to a lightly greased pizza tray.
3 Raise the edges of the dough 6mm (¼in) all round.
4 Prick the base all over with a fork.
5 Pre-heat the oven on convection 250° for 5 min.
6 Place the dish on the rack in the oven and cook on combination 250°/microwave medium for 5 min.
7 Allow to cool slightly before adding the filling of your choice.
8 Cook on convection 250° for 10 min or until the filling is brown and bubbling.

Note: *The base can be left to cool completely, then wrapped in freezer film, and stored in a deep freeze until needed. It takes approximately 3 min on microwave defrost to thaw out.*

Floured baps

900g (2lb) strong plain flour
3 teapoons salt
75g (3oz) margarine
300ml (½pt) milk
300ml (½pt) water
40g (1½oz) fresh yeast
1 teaspoon sugar

1 Sieve the flour and salt into a large mixing bowl.
2 Warm the milk and water in a jug on microwave medium for 3 min.
3 Add the yeast and sugar and stir until dissolved.
4 Make a well in the centre of the flour and pour in the liquid.
5 Mix well then knead, in the bowl, until the dough is smooth.
6 Turn out onto a floured surface and knead until elastic.

7 Transfer the dough into a clean bowl and cover with a damp tea cloth.
8 Leave to stand in a warm place for 2 hours or until the dough has doubled in size.
9 Turn the dough out onto a floured surface and knead for 3–4 min.
10 Divide into 10 baps and dust each liberally with flour.
11 Arrange the baps on the turntable of the oven allowing space between each for expansion during cooking.
12 Cook on microwave high for 5 min.

Note: *6 larger baps can be made with the same mixture. The cooking time will be the same.*

Garlic bread

1 french loaf
50g (2oz) butter
garlic salt or crushed garlic to taste
pinch dried parsley

1 Make diagonal cuts in the loaf almost to the base every 2 cm (¾in).
2 Mix the ingredients together until blended.
3 Spread a little of the garlic butter in each cut.
4 Loosely wrap the loaf in kitchen paper.
5 Pre-heat the oven on convection 250° for 5 min.
6 Place on the rack in the oven and cook on microwave high for 1½ min. Serve immediately.

Crunch biscuits

125g (5oz) butter
225g (8oz) light golden soft brown sugar
1 teaspoon vanilla essence
1 egg, size 3
225g (8oz) plain flour
1½ teaspoons baking powder
pinch salt
50g (2oz) rolled oats
25g (1oz) stoned raisins

1 Combine the butter, sugar and vanilla essence in a large mixing bowl.
2 Add the egg and beat until light and fluffy.
3 Fold in the rest of the ingredients and mix well.
4 Divide into 2 portions.
5 Roll each portion into a cylindrical shape and wrap in greaseproof paper. Refrigerate for a minimum of 3 hours.
6 Unwrap and cut each cylinder into 9 slices.
7 Lightly grease the oven turntable and pre-heat on convection 250° for 5 min.
8 Place 9 slices directly on the turntable and cook on combination 250°/microwave medium for 4) min.
9 Repeat with the second batch.

Note: *Remember to clean the grease from the turntable on completion.*

Ginger snaps

100g (4oz) butter
1 tablespoon golden syrup
225g (8oz) self-raising flour
15g (½oz) ground ginger
½ teaspoon ground cinnamon
½ teaspoon bi-carbonate of soda
25g (1oz) caster sugar
1 tablespoon milk

1 Melt the butter and syrup in a mixing bowl on microwave high for 2 min.
2 Add the other ingredients and mix well.
3 On a floured surface, roll out to a thickness of 6mm (¼in).
4 Cut out the biscuits with a medium sized pastry cutter.
5 Lightly grease the oven turntable and pre-heat on convection 250° for 5 min.
6 Divide the biscuits into two batches and place directly on the turntable. Cook on combination 250°/microwave medium for 4½ min.
7 Repeat with the second batch.

Note: *Remember to clean the turntable on completion.*

Shortbread

150g (6oz) plain flour
50g (2oz) caster sugar
100g (4oz) butter

1 Mix together the flour and sugar.
2 Rub in the butter until crumbly.
3 Press the shortbread mixture into a lightly greased rectangular Pyrex dish 20×15cm (8×6in).
4 Lightly prick with a fork.
5 Pre-heat the oven on convection 250° for 5 min.
6 Place the dish on the rack in the oven and cook on combination 250°/microwave medium for 7 min.
7 Allow to cool slightly before marking into slices with a knife.
8 Dust with caster sugar.
9 When cold, remove from the dish and break into slices.

Flapjacks

100g (4oz) demerara sugar
3 tablespoons golden syrup
100g (4oz) butter
225g (8oz) rolled oats
1 teaspoon baking powder
½ teaspoon salt
1 egg, size 3, beaten

1 Heat the sugar, syrup and butter, in a large mixing bowl, on microwave high for 4 min.
2 Remove the bowl from the oven and stir until the sugar is dissolved.
3 Add the remaining ingredients and mix well.
4 Turn the mixture into a greased 21.5cm (9in) Pyrex sponge dish and level the surface.
5 Pre-heat the oven on convection 250° for 5 min.
6 Place the dish on the rack in the oven and cook, uncovered, on combination 250°/microwave medium for 8 min.

VARIATION
Add 25g (1oz) shelled peanuts and 25g (1oz) raisins at stage 3.

Jams and preserves

If making jams and marmalades conjures up visions of huge pans, sticky hands and wasps you could be in for a pleasant surprise. Jam-making in your combination oven is a not a bit like that because smaller quantities are made quickly using easy-to-wash Pyrex casseroles. Jams need no added setting agents since there is more pectin left in the fruit due to the short cooking time. Be sure to use a large casserole to allow the sugar to boil up during cooking. Always use oven gloves when handling the hot dish. Test for setting in the normal way by dropping a little of the preserve onto a cold saucer. Place in the refrigerator for a few minutes. If a skin forms and wrinkles when pushed with a finger the setting point has been reached. Alternatively, a sugar thermometer may be used but not left in the oven during cooking. Jars can be sterilised in the oven just before filling. Wash jars thoroughly, rinse in clean water and shake out excess water. Place upside down on the turntable and heat on microwave high for 20 sec per jar or until dry. The weights given for finished jams are approximate.

Rhubarb jam *(makes 600g (1¼lb))*

450g (1lb) rhubarb
1 lemon
1 orange
225g (8oz) preserving sugar

1 Wash and trim the rhubarb. Cut into 2.5cm (1in) pieces.
2 Cook, covered, in a 2½ litre (4pt) casserole on microwave high for 6 min.
3 Wash and dry the citrus fruit. Halve and squeeze out the juice. Reserve.
4 Grate the rind of both fruits and add to the cooked rhubarb along with the juice and sugar. Stir well.
5 Cook, uncovered, on microwave high for 15 min or until setting point has been reached.
6 Leave to cool for 30 min then pot in warm jars.

Three fruit marmalade
(makes 2.8kg (5lb))

2 medium lemons
2 medium grapefruits
2 medium oranges
1.8kg (4lb) preserving sugar
900ml (1½ pts) boiling water

1 Wash and dry the fruit.
2 Cut in halves. Squeeze the juice into a 2½ litre (4pt) casserole.
3 Place the pith and pips in a muslin bag and add to the juice.
4 Shred the peel according to preference; fine, medium or thick.
5 Add the peel and 300 ml (½pt) boiling water to the juice and leave to stand for 1 hour.
6 Add the remaining 600ml (1pt) boiling water and stir in the sugar until it dissolves.
7 Cook, uncovered, on microwave high as follows:
Fine peel: 18–20 min.
Medium peel: 20–25 min.
Thick peel: 25–30 min.
8 Test if setting point has been reached. If not, continue to cook on microwave high, checking every 2 min.
9 Leave to cool for 30 min before potting in warm jars.

Lemon curd *(makes 225g (½lb))*

2 lemons
75g (3oz) unsalted butter
2 eggs, size 3
1 additional egg yolk
125g (5oz) caster sugar

1 Wash, dry and halve the lemons. Squeeze out the juice and reserve. Grate the rind finely and reserve.
2 Melt the butter, in a 2½ litre (4pt) casserole, on microwave high for 2 min.
3 Add the lemon juice and rind, eggs, additional yolk and sugar. Beat well until smooth.
4 Cook, uncovered, on microwave high for 4 min or until the curd coats the back of a spoon when tested.

Three Fruit Marmalade (above); Raspberry Jam (page 56); Lemon Curd (above)

Blackberry and apple jam
(makes 1.2kg (2¾lb))

450g (1lb) blackberries
450g (1lb) cooking apples
150ml (¼pt) water
1 kilo (2.2lb) preserving sugar

1 Husk, wash and pick-over the blackberries.
2 Peel, core and thinly slice the apples.
3 Combine the prepared fruit along with the water in a 2½ litre (4pt) casserole.
4 Cook, uncovered, on microwave high for 5 min or until the fruit is soft.
5 Stir in the sugar.
6 Cook, uncovered, on microwave high for 20 min or until the setting point is reached. Stir occasionally during cooking.
7 Leave to cool for 30 min then pot in warm jars.

Raspberry jam *(makes 450g (1lb))*

450g (1lb) raspberries
450g (1lb) preserving sugar

1 Cook the raspberries, uncovered, in a 2½ litre (4pt) casserole on microwave high for 5 min or until the fruit has softened.
2 Stir in the sugar until dissolved and cook, uncovered, for 12 min or until the setting point is reached.
3 Leave to cool for 30 min then pot in warm jars.

Green tomato chutney
(makes 1.1kg (2½lb))

450g (2lb) green tomatoes, peeled and chopped
225g (8oz) onions, peeled and chopped
1 teaspoon salt
15g (½oz) ground ginger
15g (½oz) ground cinnamon
15g (½oz) cayenne pepper
100g (4oz) brown sugar
300ml (½pt) malt vinegar

1 Combine the tomatoes, onions, salt and spices in a 2½ litre (4pt) casserole.
2 Cook, covered, on microwave high for 10 min.
3 Stir in the sugar and vinegar and cook, covered, on microwave high for 35 min or until the chutney is thick and well blended Stir occasionally during cooking.
4 Allow to cool for 30 min and pot in warm jars.

Sauces

A tasty sauce will enliven the most ordinary dish, turning a simple meal into something more exciting and appetising. Cook sauces uncovered unless otherwise specified and use a large 1.2 litre (2 pint) jug to allow room for liquids to boil and to make stirring easier. A plastic whisk, specially made for microwave ovens, can be left in the jug during cooking and this helps to avoid mess and a loss of sauce every time stirring is required. The timings are necessarily approximate because ingredients such as butter and milk taken straight from the refrigerator will take longer to heat than at room temperature.

Basic meat sauce *(serves 4)*

1 large onion, chopped
1 tablespoon cooking oil
450g (1lb) minced beef
40g (1½oz) plain flour
100g (4oz) mushrooms, finely chopped
1 clove garlic, crushed
225g (8 oz) tin chopped tomatoes
2 tablespoons tomato purée
1 bay leaf
150ml (¼pt) hot beef stock

1 Stir the onion and oil in a 1.2 litre (2pt) casserole.
2 Cook, covered, on microwave high for 3 min.
3 Stir in the minced beef.
4 Cook, covered, on microwave high for 12 min. Break up with a fork twice during cooking.
5 Drain off any excess fat.
6 Add all the remaining ingredients. Stir well.
7 Cook, covered, on microwave medium for 15 min or until the mince is fully cooked.

Note: *Serve with spaghetti or as a pancake filling. By adding 15g (½oz) plain flour to thicken further it makes an excellent pasty filling. Can be made in advance and stored in the freezer.*

Basic white sauce *(makes 300ml (½pt))*

25g (1oz) butter
25g (1oz) plain flour
300ml (½pt) milk
salt and pepper

1 Melt the butter in a jug on microwave high for 1 min.
2 Stir in the flour and gradually blend in the milk.
3 Cook on microwave high for 3 min or until the sauce has thickened. Stir every min.
4 Season with salt and pepper.

VARIATIONS
Add the extra ingredients 2 min before the end of the cooking time.
Cheese Sauce. Add 75g (3oz) grated cheese.
Mushroom Sauce. Add 50g (2oz) sliced mushrooms. Cook sauce for 1 min extra.
Onion Sauce. Add 75g (3oz) cooked chopped onion.
Parsley Sauce. Add 2 tablespoons chopped parsley.

Hunters' sauce *(serves 4)*

40g (1½oz) butter
50g (2oz) sliced mushrooms
¼ teaspoon salt
pepper
2 spring onions, chopped
1 tablespoon tomato purée
1 teaspoon chopped parsley
120ml (4fl oz) red wine
150ml (5fl oz) basic white sauce (see page 57 and halve the quantities)

1 Melt the butter in a jug on microwave high for 1½ min.
2 Add the mushrooms, seasoning, spring onions, tomato purée and parsley. Stir well.
3 Cook on microwave high for 2 min.
4 Stir in the wine and white sauce.
5 Cook on microwave high for 1 min or until hot.

Serve with chops, steaks, sausages or gammon steaks.

Thick cheese sauce *(makes 300ml (½pt))*

25g (1oz) butter
40g (1½oz) plain flour
300ml (½pt) milk
75g (2oz) grated cheese
salt and pepper

1 Melt the butter in a jug on microwave high for 1 min.
2 Stir in the flour and gradually blend in the milk.
3 Cook on microwave high for 1 min. Stir well.
4 Stir in the grated cheese.
5 Cook on microwave high for 2 min or until the sauce thickens. Stir every min.
6 Season with salt and pepper.

Bread sauce *(serves 6)*

75g (3oz) soft fresh breadcrumbs
300ml (½pt) milk
15g (½oz) butter
1 medium onion, peeled and stuck with 6 cloves
salt and pepper
2 tablespoons double cream

1 Combine all the ingredients in a jug. Stir well.
2 Cook on microwave high for 4 min.
3 Leave to stand for 5 min before removing the onion and cloves.

Serve with roast chicken or turkey.

Chocolate sauce *(makes 120ml (4fl oz))*

50g (2oz) plain chocolate
25g (1oz) butter
2 tablespoons milk

1 Break the chocolate into small pieces.
2 Place in a jug with the butter and cook on microwave high for 2 min or until melted.
3 Add the milk and stir until smooth and glossy.

Butterscotch sauce *(makes 300ml (½pt))*

50g (2oz) butter
225g (8oz) brown sugar
2 tablespoons lemon juice
60ml (2fl oz) double cream

1 Melt the butter in a jug on microwave high for 2 min.
2 Stir in all the ingredients and cook on microwave high for 3 min. Stir every min.

Note: *serve hot or cold with ice cream.*

VARIATION
Leave till cool and add an egg yolk to the sauce. Beat until smooth. Whisk the egg white to peaks. Whisk the contents of a 300ml (8oz) carton of whipping cream to a firm consistency. Fold together the egg white, cream and sauce. Turn into individual dishes and chill well. Sprinkle with demerara sugar and serve.

Fruit sauce *(makes 450ml (¾pt))*

1 tablespoon cornflour
100g (4oz) caster sugar
120ml (4fl oz) boiling water
2 tablespoons lemon juice
240ml (8fl oz) fruit juice

1 Mix the cornflour, sugar and boiling water in a jug.
2 Cook on microwave high for 3 min.
3 Allow to cool slightly.
4 Stir in the lemon juice and the fruit juice and cook on microwave high for 2 min.

Porridge (page 33); Poached Egg (page 34); Bacon (page 18); Sausages (page 17)

Fruit

The wide selection of fresh fruit available all the year round is a boon to the microwave cook. Fruit cooks quickly, retaining colour and flavour as well as the all-important vitamins we all need. The recipes chosen here are a joy to serve and easily prepared so that they can be included in everyday menu planning as well as for special occasions.

Stewed apples

450g (1lb) cooking apples
2 tablespoons sugar
1 tablespoon water

1 Peel, core and slice the apples.
2 Place the apples in a casserole and sprinkle over the sugar and water.
3 Cook, covered, on microwave high for 6 min.
4 Taste and add extra sugar if required.

ALTERNATIVE
Substitute honey for sugar. 1 tablespoon honey for 2 of sugar.

Apple bee

50g (2oz) soft margarine
50g (2oz) caster sugar
50g (2oz) self-raising flour
1 egg, size 3
1 tablespoon milk
1 large cooking apple
2 tablespoons clear honey
1 teaspoon demerara sugar

1 Mix the margarine and sugar in a bowl until light and fluffy.
2 Add the egg, 25g (1oz) of flour and the milk. Mix gently.
3 Add the remaining 25g (1oz) flour and mix until smooth.
4 Turn the mixture into a lightly greased oval pie dish and level the surface.
5 Peel, core and thinly slice the apple.
6 Arrange the apple slices evenly over the mixture.
7 Pour the honey over the apples and sprinkle with 1 tablespoon demerara sugar.
8 Pre-heat the oven on convection 250° for 5 min.
9 Place the dish on the rack in the oven and cook, uncovered, on combination 250°/microwave medium for 7 min.
10 Continue to cook on convection 250° for a further 5 min or until golden brown.

Caramelised oranges

4 medium oranges
1 tablespoon Grand Marnier or Cointreau (optional)
225g (8oz) granulated sugar
150ml (¼pt) cold water
450ml (¾pt) hot water

1 Grate the rind from 3 of the oranges and retain.
2 Peel the remaining orange and retain the peel.
3 Remove the pith and membrane from all 4 oranges.
4 Using a sharp knife, slice the oranges very thinly and arrange in a shallow dish.
5 If used, sprinkle the liqueur over the oranges.
6 Stir the sugar into the cold water in a large bowl and cook, covered, on microwave high for 15 min or until the liquid is golden brown.
7 Remove from the oven, using oven gloves, and stir in the hot water. Cook, uncovered, on microwave high for 1 min.
8 Allow the liquid to cool and during this time remove the pith from the reserved orange peel and cut into very fine shreds with a sharp knife.
9 Pour the cooled liquid over the oranges and sprinkle with the reserved grated rind. Decorate with the finely shredded peel.

Quick fruit dessert

1×450g (14oz) tin of fruit
100g (4oz) caster sugar
100g (4oz) soft margarine
2 eggs, size 3
100g (4oz) self-raising flour

1 Drain the juice and puree the fruit.
2 Mix the sugar and margarine in a bowl and beat until light and fluffy.
3 Mixing gently, add the eggs one at a time along with a little of the flour.
4 Stir in the fruit puree and the remainder of the flour.
5 Turn the mixture into a greased ring mould and level the top.
6 Cook, uncovered, on microwave high for 5–6 min. The pudding will shrink from the side of the dish when cooked.

Rhubarb crisp

450g (1lb) fresh rhubarb
150ml (¼pt) water
1 heaped teaspoon granulated sugar
225g (8oz) demerara sugar
75g (3oz) self-raising flour
100g (4oz) margarine, frozen solid and grated
75g (3oz) rolled oats

1 Trim and wash the rhubarb.
2 Cut into 2.5cm (1in) pieces and place in a Pyrex pie dish.
3 Stir in the water and granulated sugar.
4 Cook, covered, on microwave high for 4 min.
5 Combine the demerara sugar, flour, oats and grated margarine in a bowl and work together until it becomes a rough crumble.
6 Sprinkle the crumble mixture evenly over the rhubarb.
7 Cook, uncovered, on microwave high for 15 min.

ALTERNATIVE
Drain 1 large tin of rhubarb retaining 150ml (¼pt) of the juice. Add the juice and rhubarb to the casserole and follow the above recipe from stage 5.

Hot fruit compote

2 eating apples
2 dessert pears
2 bananas
2 tangerine oranges
15g (1oz) butter
30g (2oz) raisins
2 dessertspoons demerara sugar
juice of 1 lemon
juice of 1 lime
4 tablespoons fresh orange juice

1 Peel, core and thinly slice the apples and pears.
2 Peel and slice the banana.
3 Peel and remove pith from the tangerine segments.
4 Melt the butter in a large jug for 1 min.
5 Add all the other ingredients and stir well.
6 Butter a casserole and pour in the mixture.
7 Cook, covered, on microwave high for 9 min or until fruit is softened.

Note: *If red apples are used the skin may be left on for added colour.*

Bananas in rum

3 ripe bananas
2 tablespoons rum
25g (1oz) demerara sugar
¼ teaspoon ground cinnamon
15g (½oz) butter

1 Slice the bananas in half lengthways.
2 Arrange the sliced bananas in a layer in a buttered round Pyrex sponge dish.
3 Pour the rum over the bananas and sprinkle with the sugar and cinnamon.
4 Dot with the butter and allow the dish to stand for 30 min covered with kitchen paper.
5 Pre-heat the oven on convection 250° for 5 min.
6 Cook, uncovered, on combination 250°/ microwave medium for 5 min.

Note: *Rum essence, diluted with water, may be used as a substitute for the rum.*

Pears in ginger

1 lemon
75g (3oz) brown sugar
75g (3oz) granulated sugar
pinch of salt
1 teaspoon ground ginger
1 teaspoon ground cinnamon
150ml (¼pt) water
3 small, ripe dessert pears
2 tablespoons brown sugar, for sprinkling

1 Grate the lemon and squeeze the juice into a large jug.
2 Add the lemon rind, brown and granulated sugars, salt, spices and water.
3 Cook, uncovered, on microwave high for 6 min. Stir once during cooking.
4 Peel and halve the pears. Remove the core.
5 Arrange the pears, cut side down, in a rectangular pie dish and pour the syrup over. Sprinkle with 2 tablespoons brown sugar.
6 Cook, uncovered, on microwave high for 5 min.

SUBSTITUTE
Use 6 halves of tinned pears and replace the water with juice for a sweeter taste.

Stuffed baked apples

4 medium cooking apples
2 tablespoons water
4 tablespoons sweet mincemeat

1 Core the apples and score the skin around the centre with a sharp knife.
2 Add the water to a rectangular Pyrex flan dish and place the apples evenly around the outer edge.
3 Spoon 1 tablespoon of sweet mincemeat into each apple.
4 Cook, uncovered, on microwave high for 12 min.

Index

Numbers in **bold** refer to illustrations

apple bee 60
  baked, stuffed 62
  crumble 44
  dumplings, old English 38, **39**
  stewed 60

bacon rashers 18, **59**
  rolls, savoury 18
bananas in rum 61
baps, floured 52
battenburg cake **2**, 46
beef braised with onions 13
  curry 32
  roast 14, **15**
  savoury minced 16
  stew 13
beefburgers 13
biscuits, crunch 52
blackberry and apple jam 56
boiled potatoes **19**, 24
bread and butter pudding 42
bread pudding 42, **47**
  old fashioned 42
braised beef, with onions 13
bread, brown 50
  garlic 52
  sauce 58
  white 50
broccoli 24
brown bread 50
brussels sprouts 24
butterscotch sauce 58

cabbage 24
calabrese 24
caramelised oranges 61
carrots **15**, 24
casserole, chicken 20
cauliflower 24
  cheese 26, **27**
celery 24
cheese and potato pie 36
  sauce 57
  sauce, thick 58
cheesy pork bake 36
cherry coconut cake 45
Cheshire hot pot 16
chicken breasts, roast 21
  casserole 20
  fricassée 21
  parcels 22, **23**
  pepperoni 21
  roast 20
  soup, chunky 6
  spicy 20
  stuffed breast mornay 22
chilli con carne, quick 14, **27**

chocolate pear pudding 40
  sauce 58
chops, lamb 16
  pork 17
  pork, cheesy bake 36
Christmas cake, quickest ever 48
  easy-bake 49
Christmas pudding, traditional 41
chutney, green tomato 56
cod in parsley sauce 10
courgettes 24
cream of tomato soup 8
creamed eggs, savoury 34
curry, beef 32
  prawn 12
custard 38
  egg 40

date and walnut teabread 46
defrosting 5
dishes 5
dumplings 13
  old English apple 38, **39**

egg and ham surprise 36
  custard 40
eggs, creamed savoury 34
  poached 34, **59**
  scrambled 36
essential reading 4

fish
  breaded plaice fillets 9
  cakes 9
  cod in parsley sauce 10
  fingers 9
  haddock bake 10
  kippers 9
  moules marinière 10, **11**
  pie 12
  prawn curry 12
  seafood thermidor 12
  stuffed trout 10, **11**
flapjacks 53
French jam slice 44
  onion soup 6
fricassée, chicken 21
frozen sausage rolls 17
fruit cake, light 48
  rich **42**, 48
  compote, hot 61
  quick dessert 61
  sauce 58
  scones **43**, 45

gammon steak with pineapple 17
garlic bread 52
gingerbread **2**, 45
ginger snaps 53
gnocci, wholemeal, with cream
    cheese sauce 29
green tomato chutney 56

haddock bake 10
ham and egg surprise 36
  layer pudding 18, **19**
  roast 18, **19**
herb pot, Lancashire 26
hot pot, Cheshire 16
  fruit compote 61
hunter's sauce 57

jacket potatoes 28
jam, blackberry and apple 56
  raspberry **55**, 56
  rhubarb 54
  roly-poly 41
  slice, French 44

kippers 9

lamb chops 16
  roast 17
Lancashire herb pot 26
lasagne 30, **31**
leeks 24
lemon crisps 49
  curd 54, **55**
  meringue pie 40
  syllabub 38
lentil soup 8

macaroni cheese 32
marmalade, three fruit 54, **55**
measuring ingredients 5
meat
  bacon rashers 18, **59**
  beefburgers 13
  beef stew 13
  braised beef with onions 13
  Cheshire hot pot 16
  frozen sausage rolls 17
  gammon steaks with pineapple 17
  ham layer pudding 18, **19**
  lamb chops 16
  pork chops 17
  quick chilli con carne 14, **27**
  roast beef 14, **15**
    ham 18, **19**
    lamb 17
  sausages 17, **59**
  savoury bacon rolls 18
    minced beef 16
  shepherd's pie 14, **31**
  steak and kidney pudding 16
meat sauce, basic 57
meringue, mock pavlova 37
  pie, lemon 40
minced beef, savoury 16
mincemeat parcels, sweet 38
minestrone soup, quick 6, **7**
moules marinière 10, **11**
mushroom croquettes 28
  mediterranean 26
  sauce 57
  soup 8

noodles, savoury 29

old fashioned bread pudding 42
onion sauce 57
onions 24
oranges, caramelised 60

parsley sauce 57
parsnips 24
pasta and rice, hints on cooking 29
peach sponge pudding 37
pear, chocolate pudding 40
pears in ginger 62
pepperoni, chicken 21
peppers, stuffed 25, **51**
pizza base **51**, 52
plaice fillets, breaded 9
poached eggs 34, **59**
pork chops 17
porridge 33, **59**
potato and cheese pie 36
potatoes, boiled **19**, 24
    jacket 28
    scalloped **23**, 28
prawn curry 12

quiche, savoury 34, **35**
quick fruit dessert 61

raspberry jam **55**, 56
ratatouille 26, **51**
rhubarb crisp **39**, 61
    jam 54
rice pudding, traditional 32
    salad, savoury 33, **35**
risotto, Milano 32
roast beef 14, **15**
    chicken 20
        breasts 21
    crown of lamb 17
    ham 18, **19**
    lamb 17
roly-poly, jam 41
runner beans 24
ruotine 30

sauces
    basic meat 57
    basic white 57
    bread 58
    butterscotch 58
    cheese 57
        thick 58
    chocolate 58
    fruit 58
    hunter's 57
    mushroom 57
    onion 57
    parsley 57
sausages 17, **59**
sausage rolls, frozen 17

savoury bacon rolls 18
    minced beef 16
scalloped potatoes **23**, 28
    sweetcorn 25
scones, fruit **43**, 45
scrambled eggs 36
seafood thermidor 12
selecting mode 4
shepherd's pie 14, **31**
shortbread 53
soups
    chunky chicken 6
    cream of tomato 8
    French onion 6
    lentil 8
    mushroom 8
    quick minestrone 6, **7**
spaghetti 30
spicy chicken 20
standing time 4
steak and kidney pudding 16
steamed sponge pudding 37
stew, beef 13
stewed apples 60
stir-fry vegetables 25
strawberry affairé **cover**, 41
stuffed baked apples 62
    chicken mornay 22
    peppers 25, **51**
    trout 10, **11**
sweetcorn, scalloped 25
syllabub, lemon 38

tagliatelle, parmesan 29
teabread, date and walnut 46
thick cheese sauce 58
trout, stuffed 10, **11**
turnips 24

vegetables
    broccoli 24
    brussels sprouts 24
    cabbage 24
    calabrese 24
    carrots **15**, 24
    cauliflower 24
        cheese 26, **27**
    celery 24
    cooking hints 24
    courgettes 24
    jacket potatoes 28
    Lancashire herb pot 26
    mushroom croquettes 28
        mediterranean 26
    parsnips 24
    peppers, stuffed 25
    potatoes, boiled **19**, 24
        scalloped **23**, 28
    ratatouille 26, **51**
    runner beans 24
    stir-fry vegetables 25

sweetcorn, scalloped 25
turnips 24

Victorian sandwich 46, **47**

white bread 50
white sauce, basic 57

Yorkshire pudding 14, **15**

Acknowledgements

Photography: Charles Parsons

Typesetting:
Ace Filmsetting, Frome

Colour separations:
Columbia Offset, Singapore

Printing and binding:
Royal Smeets Offset b.v., Weert

© 1989 Jan Harris

Printed in the Netherlands for Angell Editions Limited
39 Coombeshead Road
Newton Abbot, Devon

British Library Cataloguing in Publication Data

Harris, Jan
    Introducing microwave combination cookery.
    1. Food, Dishes prepared using microwave ovens –
    Recipes
    I. Title
    641.5′882

ISBN 0 948432 65 9